Open for Debate
Workers' Rights

make the
Global
Economy
WORK
for working
families

AFL-CIO

經理
取百萬資口
人工重
足餉口
老闆！
你有冇冇關

STOP
Corpo
GRE
Jobs with J

GAP!
YOUR LABEL
Your Responsibility
What About
WORKERS?

make
Global
Econo
WO
for wor
fam

GAP
Earn
WO
Ear
H

H
G
WI /
W RH

AFL CIO

Open for Debate
Workers' Rights

Richard Worth

Marshall Cavendish
Benchmark
New York

With thanks to Esta R. Bigler,
director of the law and employment law programs
at Cornell University, New York,
for her expert review of this manuscript.

Marshall Cavendish Benchmark
99 White Plains Road
Tarrytown, NY 10591
www.marshallcavendish.us
Copyright © 2008 by Marshall Cavendish Corporation

All Internet sites were available and accurate when sent to press.

Library of Congress Cataloging-in-Publication Data
Worth, Richard.
Workers' rights / by Richard Worth.
p. cm. — (Open for debate)
Summary: "Traces the history of workers' rights and labor law in America
through to the present day, including detailed analysis of labor unions,
discrimination, safety, the rights of immigrant workers, and other issues in
the workplace"—Provided by publisher.
Includes bibliographical references and index.
ISBN 978-0-7614-2574-8
1. Labor laws and legislation—United States. 2. Labor laws and
legislation—United States—History. 3. Employee rights—United States. I.
Title. II. Series.
KF3319.6.W67 2007
344.730109—dc22
2007000290

Photo research by Lindsay Aveilhe and Linda Sykes/
Linda Sykes Picture Research, Inc., Hilton Head, SC

AP/Wide World Photos: cover, 2–3, 11, 52, 84, 86, 93, 103;
Chris Stewart/CORBIS: 6; The Granger Collection: 23, 30;
© Bettmann/CORBIS: 37, 44; Owen Franken/CORBIS: 53;
© Ron Sachs/CNP/CORBIS: 65; © CORBIS: 79; © Ken Cedeno/CORBIS: 106.

Publisher: Michelle Bisson
Art Director: Anahid Hamparian
Series Designer: Sonia Chaghatzbanian

Printed in China

1 3 5 6 4 2

Contents

BETTY DUKES, 53, STARTED A CLASS-ACTION SUIT AGAINST WAL-MART IN 2004,
ALLEGING THAT THE GIANT STORE CHAIN DISCRIMINATED AGAINST FEMALE EMPLOYEES.

1
Workers at
Wal-Mart

Betty Dukes went to work for a Wal-Mart store, located in Pittsburg, California, in 1994. Dukes, an African American, started as a cashier, working at one of the checkout counters, for which she was paid five dollars per hour. Because of her hard work and attention to detail, she was eventually promoted to the position of customer-service manager. Dukes hoped that this was only the beginning of her career promotions at Wal-Mart. But she was disappointed. Each time she applied for a training program so she could advance to the next level, Dukes was turned down by her boss. Instead, men were given the openings in the training program, as well as the promotions that she believed belonged to her. Dukes complained to her boss. Soon afterward she lost her position as customer-service manager and was moved back to her old job as a cashier. Eventually, she lost this job and was demoted to a position greeting customers as they entered the store. Her pay was so low that she had to hold down two other jobs to support herself.

In 2000 Betty Dukes decided to sue Wal-Mart for sex discrimination. Specifically, she sued the company under Title VII of the 1964 Civil Rights Act. This act states that employees shall not face discrimination because of their sex, race, religion, or national origin. She claimed that the store unfairly denied her promotions, giving them instead to men. Dukes also charged that she had faced discrimination because she was an African American.

Soon afterward Betty Dukes discovered that other women had received the same treatment at Wal-Mart. They were denied promotions or paid less than men in the same jobs. Managers claimed that men were supporting families and therefore deserved promotions and higher salaries. Among the women who said they experienced discrimination was Christine Kwapnoski. She worked in a Wal-Mart store located in Concord, California. For her outstanding performance, Kwapnoski was repeatedly named "associate of the month." But she was never permitted to participate in the store's management training program. Deborah Gunter joined Wal-Mart in Riverside, California, in 1996, working for $5.50 per hour in the store's photo laboratory. Gunter had raised dogs for many years and wanted to run the store's pet department. But each time she applied for the job, Gunter was turned down. Instead, teenage boys—with no experience working with animals—were appointed in her place.

In 2004 Kwapnoski, Gunter, and 1.6 million other female Wal-Mart employees joined Betty Dukes in a class action suit against the giant retail chain. A class action suit occurs when a group of people with the same grievance join together to sue a defendant. *Dukes* v. *Wal-Mart* is the largest class action suit ever brought to the U.S. court system. As Betty Dukes said, it was "like David versus Goliath."

Wal-Mart and Its Global Reach

Wal-Mart is indeed the Goliath of the retail industry—it is the largest retailer in the world. There are over 3,500 stores located in the United States and around the globe. Although Wal-Mart's headquarters are located in Bentonville, Arkansas, most of its suppliers are based in China. Salaries are low in China, and products can be produced very cheaply. Indeed, as much as $30 billion of Wal-Mart's imports may come from Chinese factories annually. As one of the company's executives explained, "We do depend on products from around the globe to draw our consumers into the stores. We feel they need to have the best product, the best value, at the best price we can achieve." Customers worldwide expect the same thing or they won't shop at Wal-Mart.

Wal-Mart is an American success story. Founded by entrepreneur Sam Walton, it has transformed the retail industry. According to economist Brink Lindsey of the conservative Cato Institute, "Wal-Mart is good for America. Wal-Mart is doing what the American economy is all about, which is producing things consumers want to buy . . . offering a wide range of goods at rock-bottom prices." Wal-Mart has achieved its success by its sheer size. It has become the largest seller of a variety of products—from food items to clothes, appliances, and toys. In some cases Wal-Mart accounts for as much as 40 percent of the entire market in some of these goods. Manufacturing companies in these fields must sell to Wal-Mart or risk going out of business. Therefore, Wal-Mart can dictate low prices and pass them along to consumers. This helps allow customers with low incomes to buy what they need.

The chain also knows what its patrons want to buy. A bar code on each item is read by a computer at the cash register. "When they scan that in when you buy it," explains University of California sociology professor Edna Bonacich, "that information is immediately collected [by Wal-Mart. So] . . . they know the brand name and so forth. All of that is put into the [Wal-Mart] information system. And then, if you have a good partnership with your vendor, that [information] is beamed down to them, and they know [what] has sold. They know, 'We need to reproduce this.'" Giving consumers only what they want at "everyday low prices" allows Wal-Mart to dominate the consumer products industry. As one shopper put it, "Who doesn't shop at Wal-Mart? You can't beat their prices."

Wal-Mart keeps its prices low by being a low-cost operator—that is, it pays employees low wages with few benefits. By keeping prices down, Wal-Mart helps keep inflation low, according to some economists. This helps to strengthen the American economy and keeps retail business booming.

The Global Marketplace

Over the past century, the American economy has become part of a global marketplace. Companies in the United States have closed down manufacturing plants and shipped jobs overseas. In Asia and Latin America, wages are lower, workers are forced to stay at their jobs for long hours, and products can be manufactured at lower costs. Consumers want inexpensive items but do not often ask themselves why these items are so cheap. Indeed, most American consumers expect to go into discount stores like Wal-Mart and buy inexpensive clothing, appliances, sporting goods, and other products. For retailers to compete, they must keep prices and the cost of their operations very low. Wal-Mart is one example of a low-cost operator, but there have been many others, such as McDonald's or Costco. However, low prices for consumers often conflict with the rights of workers.

BY 2007, WAL-MART OPERATED MORE THAN SEVENTY STORES
EMPLOYING ABOUT 35,000 PEOPLE IN CHINA. A WORKER IN
SHANGHAI CLEANS A WALL AROUND A PICTURE OF THE CHAIN'S
FOUNDER, SAM WALTON.

The Other Side of "Everyday Low Prices"

Each individual is not only a consumer but also a worker.
"If people were only consumers, buying things at lower
prices would be just good," says economist Larry Mishel.
"But people also are workers who need to earn a decent
standard of living. The dynamics that create lower prices

at Wal-Mart and other places are also undercutting the ability of many, many workers to earn decent wages and benefits and have a stable life."

One of these workers is Betty Dukes, but there are many others as well. Some are women. Statistics indicate that 65 percent of cashiers and greeters— low-paying jobs—are filled by women at Wal-Mart. In contrast, only 35 percent of assistant managers are women, even though they make up more than 70 percent of Wal-Mart employees. In addition, women are paid less than men for the same jobs. These include positions as cashiers and greeters, as well as managers. This wage discrimination helps keep prices low—serving the needs of consumers who demand and expect low prices.

Wal-Mart has tried to keep prices low in other ways, too. In 2005 hourly workers at Wal-Mart stores in Missouri brought a class action suit against the retailer, charging that they had not received overtime pay. In addition, the employees had to work through lunch breaks and rest breaks. A similar class action suit was brought in Pennsylvania in 2006. The workers won $78.4 million from Wal-Mart in court. Meanwhile, Wal-Mart faced yet another suit brought by illegal immigrants. They accused the retailer of not remitting the overtime pay due to them for cleaning the floors. Wal-Mart claimed that U.S. law should not apply to the workers because they had entered the country illegally. But District Judge Joseph Greenaway said that their status did not affect the case. As the judge put it, "This court only joins a growing chorus acknowledging the right of workers to seek relief for work already performed." As a result, the case went forward.

Wal-Mart's activities strike at the foundation of workers' rights in the United States. In addition to issues of sex and race discrimination and employing illegal immigrants, the retailer has also fought a long battle to stop unions from entering its stores to represent workers.

Unions push for higher wages and benefits for their members. By keeping unions out, Wal-Mart has not only kept its own prices low but has also made a major impact on working conditions at other large retail chains. In supermarkets, for example, where many workers are unionized, management has tried to lower prices to compete with prices at Wal-Mart. This has often meant trying to force unionized workers to accept cuts in their salaries.

The struggles at Wal-Mart and other retailers focus attention on many important issues regarding the rights of Americans as employees in the workplace. These issues include:

- **What role should unions play in the modern consumer marketplace, balancing workers' rights against the rights of employers and consumers?**

- **How should the law protect women against sex discrimination and minorities against racial discrimination by an employer?**

- **What benefits—such as health care and retirement health insurance—should workers receive, including gay and lesbian employees and their partners?**

- **What constitutes legal treatment for older workers and disabled employees?**

- **How should employers balance the safety of their employees against the desire to make a profit?**

- **What rights should immigrant workers have under U.S. law?**

The Role of Unions

The global marketplace has helped undermine the role of American labor unions. Most workers are employed "at will," that is, they can be fired at the will of employers for no cause whatsoever. Unions fought to achieve protection for workers from unfair employers, as well as better pay, shorter working hours, and fair benefits. But by the last part of the twentieth century, more and more companies were moving jobs overseas. This gave them a means of combating the demands of unions. In addition, some unions were run by corrupt officials who had fattened their own pocketbooks at the expense of their members. By the early twenty-first century, only about 8 percent of American workers in the private sector belonged to unions. Not surprisingly, with the decline of unions, the rights of workers were no longer as well protected as they had been in the past.

Rights of Minorities and Women

Although African Americans were freed from slavery in the 1860s, they faced severe racial discrimination for another century. They were prevented from holding many types of jobs, barred from joining unions, and treated as second-class citizens. With the passage of the Civil Rights Act of 1964, discrimination against racial minorities in the workplace was prohibited by law. African Americans began to fill more and more jobs that had been closed to them in the past. Many companies also developed affirmative action programs, creating goals to hire a certain percentage of minorities. But these programs created controversy when white workers accused their employers of practicing reverse discrimination.

Women had also faced years of discrimination in the workplace, but that lessened with the passage of the Civil

14

Rights Act. Hundreds of thousands of women entered jobs that had been closed to them in the past. Nevertheless, they still dealt with sexual harassment, which was eventually prohibited, but not eliminated, with the passage of new laws.

Protecting Workers' Benefits

As a result of union pressure, many new employee contracts incorporated significant benefit packages, including vacations, workers' compensation, and health care. However, as the cost of health care increased, many companies eliminated health benefits for retirees and required employees to pay more for their health insurance. Many employees, especially low-paid workers, lack any benefits and are among more than 46 million Americans who do not have any health insurance. On the one hand, higher pay and health benefits would create an extra burden for employers. With higher financial obligations to their workers, these companies would be forced to charge higher prices for their products, creating an extra burden for many of their customers with limited incomes. On the other hand, low pay and no health benefits create an enormous problem for many employees who cannot afford medical care, decent housing, or other basic necessities. It also places a tremendous burden on hospitals that must treat patients without health insurance.

The Rights of Older and Disabled Workers

The rights of older workers and the disabled are protected by federal and state laws. Nevertheless, these laws do not always stop an employee's rights from being violated in the workplace. Proving age discrimination, for example, is often very difficult. Many employees are not willing to take on a powerful employer with huge financial resources. They are afraid of losing their jobs and often lack the knowledge or the money to sue. The disabled may also face discrimination in the workplace. Wal-Mart recently lost a lawsuit brought by two former employees who charged the retailer with discrimination because they were deaf. Some of these court cases, however, are clearly without foundation. They may be initiated by employees who are trying to win large financial rewards from their employers. Finding a balance that protects the worker and the employer is often extremely difficult.

Protecting Employee Safety

Federal legislation, such as the Occupational Safety and Health Act (OSHA) is designed to provide employees with a safe working environment. Yet some employers systematically violate OSHA laws, and the declining number of federal inspectors means that safety regulations are not always enforced. New efforts are currently under way by federal agencies to strengthen OSHA regulations. Meanwhile, courts are investigating dishonest claims submitted by some workers who have asserted that their health and safety were jeopardized in the workplace.

Illegal Immigrant Workers

Among the most controversial issues in the U.S. workplace are the rights of illegal immigrant workers. Millions of these workers cross the borders into the United States each year. They are often paid very poorly precisely because they have entered the United States illegally and cannot protest against the practices of their employers. Some economists have charged that these illegal immigrants are lowering wages for many American workers. Political leaders claim that illegal immigrants are using welfare programs and sending their children to schools—unfairly taking advantage of government services. Yet studies also show that these illegal immigrants are essential to the American economy. Without them, consumers could not enjoy such a large variety of low-cost products in their supermarkets.

The issue of workers' rights involves a variety of controversial questions, affecting many employees who may include your friends, your family, and even yourself.

2
Workers' Rights and the Labor Unions

The struggle for workers' rights began during the late eighteenth century. Today we take an eight-hour working day for granted. But in the past people were accustomed to working much longer. During the 1790s, for example, the average workday was twelve to sixteen hours. In 1791 carpenters in Philadelphia, Pennsylvania, went on strike for a shorter working day. They demanded a twelve-hour day, including ten hours of work and two hours off for meals—breakfast and dinner. "They will work from six to six—how absurd!" remarked a local Philadelphia newspaper. The strike failed and the carpenters eventually went back to work.

In 1806 Philadelphia became the setting for a milestone in the history of the labor struggle. Journeymen cordwainers—apprentice shoemakers—had joined together throughout the city to strike for higher wages. Their employers opposed any change in working conditions. The employers brought the cordwainers to court and charged them with conspiracy. That is, the shoemakers were prosecuted by their employers for illegally joining together to control wages. The employers won their case, setting a precedent for other strikes. Each time workers joined together to protest working conditions, they could be found guilty of illegal action. In New York City, hat-makers ran into the same situation in 1823. When they went on strike, they were found guilty of conspiracy. Without strikes, employees possessed little power to achieve greater rights in the workplace.

As far as employers were concerned, strikes by employee groups violated the freedom that every citizen in the United States was supposed to enjoy. Americans were not only given freedom of speech and freedom of the press, they were also supposed to have economic freedom. In other words, employers should be free to run their businesses the way that they wanted. Without this freedom, employers believed, they could not control the costs of their operations, especially the wages paid to their workers. In addition, they could not require these workers to put in long days and produce a large number of products. As a result, employers could not compete with other businesses operating in the marketplace—businesses in the same city or in other cities.

Nevertheless, employees did not give up their efforts to improve working conditions. In Dover, New Hampshire, for example, women went on strike at the Cocheco Mill in 1828. They protested the fact that the company was trying to fine the workers 12.5 cents each time they came in late. Their employer also prohibited them from talking during working hours. The strike worked and the Cocheco Mill owner eliminated the new rules.

During the 1840s other changes began to occur that provided workers with additional rights. In 1840, for example, U.S. President Martin Van Buren decided that employees of the federal government should have a ten-hour workday. Several states followed the federal government, making ten the maximum number of hours that employees could work each day. Finally, in 1842 Massachusetts courts ruled that labor unions were not illegal—that is, they were not conspiracies against employers.

Harsh Working Conditions

While laws began to change, employees still faced harsh working conditions. During the last half of the nineteenth century, more and more people were employed in large mills. Inside each mill were huge machines run by hundreds of workers. These power looms wove cotton into cloth that was used to make clothing. Other mills turned out shoes, as many as 2,400 pairs per day. By mass-producing so many shoes, employers could keep the costs of their products low and make large profits when the items were sold.

For the mill employees, however, working conditions inside the mills were harsh. The machines were dangerous to run, and workers who caught a hand or a foot inside a power loom weaving cotton cloth could be severely injured. Employers did not provide any medical insurance. The mills employed not only men, but women and children as well. They were paid less than the male workers, which was the primary reason that mill owners employed them. There were no laws prohibiting child labor, and many children were working in factories by the age of ten. As one laborer in a shoe factory recalled,

I have seen small children standing on boxes because they were not tall enough to stand up to a man's work and operate machines. . . . the introduction of child labor is quite a factor, sometimes displacing the head of a family. There was an instance in Marlboro [Massachusetts] where a man [was] receiving $2 a day, [and] the firm turned him off and put in his own son at $1, on the same job.

In 1867 shoemakers in the Northeast formed the Order of the Knights of Saint Crispin. This labor union was named after the patron saint of shoemakers, Saint Crispin. By 1870 the union had 50,000 members. In Lynn, Massachusetts, women shoe stitchers formed the Daughters of Saint Crispin in 1869. This is considered the first national union of women. Women also joined the Typographers' Union, which represented printers, as well as the Collar Laundry Union. These women worked in laundries that washed the detachable collars from men's shirts.

Many women also joined the Knights of Labor. Formed in 1869, the Knights of Labor was considered the first important national union in the United States. Over the next two decades, membership in the Knights grew to 700,000 workers. Led by Uriah S. Stephens, the Knights enrolled workers in a variety of industries. These included railroad workers, steel workers, machinists, and blacksmiths. In 1871 the Knights supported a strike by the Daughters of Saint Crispin and pressured employers to rehire the strikers. The Knights also believed that women should receive equal pay with men—this was a revolutionary concept at that time and remained so for another century.

Although the Knights were at first successful, they failed to make major changes in the workplace. When the Knights used the strike to improve working conditions, large steel manufacturers and railroads resorted to a lockout. They refused to negotiate with workers or let them return to work. Employers also hired "scabs"—nonunion employees—to run the mills or the railroads during a strike. Eventually, many workers returned to the job without achieving their goals. They could not afford to stay out on strike and continue to feed their families.

As the Knights declined, another labor organization arose to take its place. Known as the American Federation of Labor (AFL), it was formed by a variety of craft unions

Terence V. Powderly and the Knights of Labor

Born in 1849 in Carbondale, Pennsylvania, Terence Powderly went to work on the railroads when he was only thirteen. Later he became a machinist and a member of the Machinists' and Blacksmiths' Union. After joining the Knights of Labor in 1874, Powderly demonstrated unusual leadership capabilities and was named grand master workman—or head—of the union in 1879. Powderly helped increase the membership of the Knights during the next decade. However, the group's growing power brought strong opposition from manufacturers. The Knights were demanding a shorter workday—eight hours—for the same pay as a ten-hour day. Most employers were unwilling to grant this request. During the 1880s the Knights led numerous strikes that involved thousands of workers. More than nine thousand railroad workers struck during construction of the Missouri-Pacific Railroad in March 1886. Later that year violence broke out at a gathering of workers in Haymarket Square, Chicago. When police tried to break up the meeting, a bomb was thrown, killing seven policemen. Eight men were later charged with the crime and given the death penalty. The Haymarket Riot frightened many Americans. In addition, the strikes failed to persuade large employers to improve working conditions. As a result, membership in the Knights declined. Powderly finally resigned from the Knights in 1893. He spent the rest of his career working as a lawyer and holding several government jobs. Powderly died in 1924.

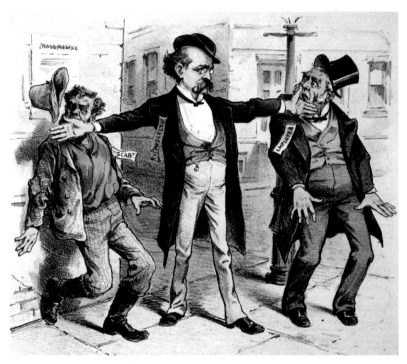

In this **1866** cartoon by Joseph Keppler, Terence V. Powderly gives the back of each hand to a scab (*LEFT*) and an employer.

in various industries in 1881. Led by Samuel Gompers, the AFL reached a membership of 500,000 by the beginning of the twentieth century. Meanwhile, violent strikes continued to break out across the United States. Unions were not only demanding higher pay and shorter hours for their members, but they also wanted what was known as a closed shop, which meant that only union workers would be allowed to work for an employer. Union leaders believed that this was the only way that their workers would present a united front against an employer's demands. However, employers believed that this gave the unions control over the workplace by taking hiring decisions out of the employer's hands.

In 1892 a strike broke out at the Homestead steel mill in Pennsylvania. A clash between strikers and guards at the mill who were trying to bring in scabs led to the deaths of almost twenty people. Strikes also broke out in the coal mines, which supplied the fuel that heated homes throughout the United States. During a strike in Verdon, Illinois, in 1898, mine owners also tried to bring in scabs. A violent clash with striking miners resulted in twenty-five deaths. Often the strikers also faced opposition from federal and state governments, which brought in troops to defend the rights of employers. In addition, the U.S. Supreme Court ruled that employers could fire workers for union activities. The combined power of the Supreme Court and government officials severely undercut the power of the unions.

Unions in the Early Twentieth Century

By the early twentieth century, unions faced a new challenge. Large manufacturers were bringing in machines to do the jobs that had required hundreds of workers. In the steel industry, for example, men who worked on furnaces were replaced by steel furnaces that ran automatically and

Samuel Gompers

Born in England in 1850, Samuel Gompers came to the United States with his family in 1863. As a teenager, he followed his father into the cigar-making industry. Gompers was employed as a reader—someone who read books to the workers while they rolled cigars. He also participated in what he called public debating societies, which discussed the rights of workers. The employees were members of the Cigar Makers' International Union. However, the union seemed incapable of improving wages or reducing hours for workers. As a result, it disappeared in 1877. Gompers and an associate, Adolph Strasser, were committed to improving working conditions, so they created a new union. As Gompers put it, "the time has come when we must assert our rights as workingmen." Gompers believed that only a strong union could prevent employers from reducing wages whenever they wanted. "To make the employees equal in power and influence to the employer, they must be organized." In 1881 Gompers became a founder of the Organized Trades and Labor Unions, reorganized as the American Federation of Labor (AFL) in 1886. He continued to lead the AFL throughout the first part of the twentieth century. During that period the union staged numerous strikes against large employers. Gompers helped achieve a shorter workday for union members, as well as higher pay. He died in 1924.

needed fewer workers to monitor them. In the cigar-making industry, people employed as rollers were replaced by cigar-rolling machines. And in the automobile industry, large manufacturers like Ford Motor Company introduced the assembly line. The total efficiency increased enormously, with automobile production rising by 400 percent and paper production by the same amount. But the worker had become part of a machine. Describing the automobile assembly line, one observer said, "day after day, year after year. . . . The pace never varies. The man is part of the chain, the feeder and the slave of it."

Workers were pushed by their supervisors to do more and more, to work faster and faster, and to keep the assembly line moving. Speed led to greater productivity, so a larger number of automobiles and other products could be made at relatively low prices for consumers and at high profits for manufacturers. But for workers, wages remained low. In many families, women as well as men had to work to earn enough money to buy food and clothing and afford a place to live.

The rapid, repetitive work became too much for some employees, who simply walked off their jobs. Employee turnover at the Ford plant in the early twentieth century was over 300 percent. As a result, Ford offered to pay its workers five dollars per hour—double the average hourly wage—to keep them working. In addition, working conditions were often unsafe, leading to many injuries and deaths. Over a fifty-year period, from 1870 to 1920, more than 75,000 coal miners died in mine accidents, such as cave-ins. Hundreds of workers in chemical industries developed lead poisoning; on the railroads, 86,000 workers were killed between 1890 and 1920.

Many workers tried to organize unions or join them, but large employers fought the organizing effort with every means available. As a result, violent conflicts broke out in many industries, and union organizers were driven out of the workplace. In addition, the courts backed the large employers by ruling that so-called yellow-dog contracts—which prohibited workers from joining unions if they wanted to remain employed—were legal.

Nevertheless, the union movement continued. In 1910, 20,000 women who belonged to the International Ladies' Garment Workers' Union (ILGWU) went on strike. Women worked long hours for very low wages in the garment industry, in hot, dusty, poorly lit sweatshops. The ILGWU forced the garment makers to recognize the union and provide its workers with higher wages, as well as improved working conditions.

World War I

In 1914 World War I broke out in Europe between the Allies—Great Britain, France, and Russia—and the Central powers—Germany and Austria-Hungary. The United States began shipping military arms and other supplies across the Atlantic Ocean to the Allies. The demand for workers increased as the economy boomed. Because they needed workers desperately, employers were more willing to permit their employees to join unions. Union membership almost doubled, to five million employees, by 1920. Union demands for higher wages and better working conditions continued; numerous strikes broke out when employers refused to meet union demands.

In 1917 the United States declared war on the Central Powers. Many male workers were recruited into the armed forces, so women often took their jobs. In the late nineteenth century, women had already entered the workforce as telephone operators and secretaries. During the war they also went to work on railroads, in manufacturing plants, and in machine shops. Meanwhile, thousands of

African Americans left their jobs on farms in the South for better-paying work in the manufacturing plants of the North. However, women and black workers faced hostility from white male employees who did not want to work side by side with them. In addition, African Americans frequently encountered discrimination from unions that prevented them from becoming members.

After World War I ended, soldiers returned home and women were forced to give up the jobs that they had filled during the war. As the need for armaments had stopped for the time being, the United States experienced a severe economic slowdown. Thousands of workers were thrown out of their jobs, leading to a steep decline in union membership. Prosperity returned during the 1920s, which pushed up wages, at least for some workers. At Ford, for example, workers received over $1,700 per year in salary. But this was far higher than the pay for most employees. Approximately 20 percent earned less than $1,000 annually, while over 40 percent made under $1,500.

The Great Depression

Conditions for American workers grew even worse after 1929, when the United States entered the Great Depression. By the early 1930s approximately 25 percent of the workforce was unemployed. At first, unions were hit hard because their members could no longer afford to pay the dues that were required. With these dues, unions had been able to support their workers during strikes. As one union leader explained, "The only thing the unions can do during these times is to hang on . . . and try to save our organization."

But as the Great Depression continued, workers began to realize that they needed to organize and act to safeguard their futures. In 1932 a majority of American voters decided to replace Republican President Herbert Hoover, and voted for a Democrat, Franklin D. Roosevelt. President Roosevelt was committed to putting people back to work with the help of new government legislation. Among the Roosevelt administration's programs was the National Industrial Recovery Act (NIRA), passed in June 1933. One of its provisions expressly supported the right of employees to join unions and bargain with employers for better wages and working conditions. The NIRA helped spur an enormous increase in union membership, especially among such organizations as the United Mine Workers and the ILGWU. Growth also occurred in other areas, such as the steel industry and the pulp and paper industry.

Nevertheless, employers continued to resist union-organizing efforts, leading to massive strikes. In addition, employers fired union activists to prevent them from recruiting new members. The NIRA lacked the strength to police every industry and prevent employers from disregarding the law. But in 1935 Congress passed tougher legislation to support the unions. Known as the Wagner Act, it was named after its sponsor, New York Senator Robert F. Wagner. Wagner believed that if unions could help improve employee wages, giving workers more money to spend, the economy might begin to rise out of the Depression. The new legislation established the National Labor Relations Board (NLRB), which had the power to investigate employers who tried to prevent union-organizing activities.

According to labor historians Robert Zieger and Gilbert Gall, the Wagner Act "was one of the seminal enactments in American history. . . . It shifted the focus of labor conflict away from violent confrontation toward the hearing rooms and courts. Prior to the passage of the Wagner Act, literally hundreds of workers had been killed and thousands injured in a long history of disputes stretching back into the nineteenth century. After its enactment . . . deaths and serious injuries in labor disputes became rare."

Don't Go In! ▸ STOP!

Strike Today!

Model Blouse Employees are ON STRIKE to end firing of UNION members, for JUST hours, FAIR wages, and DECENT working conditions!

★★★

ALL OUT ON THE PICKET LINE FOR A COMPLETE

UNION VICTORY

Amalgamated Clothing Workers of America
19 E. Pine Street, Millville, N. J.
license no. 24

IN THE EARLY TWENTIETH CENTURY, UNIONS STRUGGLED JUST FOR THE RIGHT TO EXIST. IN 1935, THE AMALGAMATED CLOTHING WORKERS CREATED THIS POSTER FOR THEIR PICKET LINE.

The passage of the Wagner Act led to a burst of union organizing activity. Union membership grew and new organizations began to form. The AFL, America's largest union, had focused much of its efforts on organizing skilled workers, such as electricians and carpenters. But some leaders, including John L. Lewis, head of the United Mine Workers, believed that it should focus far more attention on organizing unskilled workers, such as those who manned the automobile assembly lines. These leaders broke with the AFL in 1935 and formed the Committee for Industrial Organization, later known as the Congress of Industrial Organizations (CIO). Among its members were the steel workers' unions and the United Auto Workers (UAW).

Beginning late in 1936 the UAW led strikes against General Motors and Ford automakers. Thousands of workers participated in sit-down strikes—refusing to operate their machines or leave the plants. Although local police tried to remove the auto employees, they resisted and the UAW won the right to represent the workers. Similar victories occurred in the steel industry.

Unions were also beginning to force companies to give up their long-held belief that employees worked only "at will"—without job security—and could be fired at any time. Union contracts spelled out employee wages and benefits and provided protection against unfair treatment. Many employers were afraid to resist because the American economy was recovering, and large manufacturers could not afford to have their plants shut down and lose desperately needed business.

Social Security Act

While unions were trying to achieve more rights for workers, the Roosevelt administration was passing new legislation to help protect them. In 1935 Congress passed the Social Security Act. One part of the act established an old-age benefit for retired workers. At first, it was a small pension, amounting to only a few dollars per month. But over the next decades, the size of the retirement pension would grow. The money would come from contributions by employees—taken out of their paychecks—and employers, and be transferred to a social security fund. In addition, the new act provided grants to the states so that they could provide unemployment benefits to workers who had lost their jobs. This was the first time that the federal government had provided such protection for American workers.

World War II

Although American business was beginning to improve, employee wages still remained low. In 1939, for example, an average worker made only $1,250 per year. The pace of work remained nonstop and workers were regularly being intimidated by their supervisors on the factory floor—driven to work harder and faster to produce more products. Ford, for instance, employed a service department that was expected to frighten workers into doing what the company demanded of them. "Shaking 'em up in the aisles was a standard practice," workers said. "On occasion Servicemen would beat and even flog employees. . . . Conversation and even smiling became dangerous." However, the victories by the UAW at Ford began to change working conditions and push up wages.

The American economy received an enormous boost after 1939, when World War II broke out in Europe. In September, Nazi Germany invaded Poland, touching off a brutal conflict that would rage over the next six years. At first, the United States remained neutral. But the Roosevelt administration began sending supplies to the Allies—Great Britain and France—who were fighting against the Nazis. As the demand for war matériel increased, American industries began filling the orders. In December 1941 Japan attacked the United States naval base at Pearl Harbor, Hawaii, bringing America into the war in support of the Allies. As manufacturers stepped up their production of armaments, the demand for employees rose, and with it, the level of workers' wages.

To carry out the war effort, the government drafted hundreds of thousands of men into the armed services. Women, who would comprise almost 40 percent of the American workforce by the end of the war in 1945, replaced them in the factories. Nevertheless, women faced serious problems on the factory floor. As they had in World War I, women encountered resentment from men. They were prevented from entering some occupations, such as welding, that involved long apprenticeships. They were also paid less than men for the same jobs. In addition, women faced sexual harassment—"including outright physical abuse, snide innuendo [remarks], and . . . assignment of women to particularly noisome or arduous labor," according to historians Robert Zieger and Gilbert Gall. The unions did very little to help them. They regarded these issues as "a women's problem."

Black workers also faced discrimination. Many unions looked the other way and did nothing to stop it; they also barred African Americans from union membership. But the powerful UAW was an exception. At one automotive company, white workers who belonged to the UAW walked off the job and hurled threats at African Americans after management hired them. The UAW leadership stepped in, ordered the workers back to work, and barred members who practiced discrimination from the factory floor. But African Americans were routinely paid only about 50 percent of what white workers received for the same jobs.

The Postwar Period

By the end of World War II, union membership had grown to an estimated 35 percent of the American workforce. On the factory floor, union representatives routinely intervened when workers complained of unfair treatment by a supervisor. Some employees even refused to take orders from supervisors, jeopardizing work routines. This angered many employers who believed that the unions had become far too powerful. Moreover, some unions had gained a bad reputation for their activities. Leaders of the Teamsters, who organized truck drivers, were guilty of corruption and maintaining close relationships with organized crime. The Teamsters and other unions also resorted to strong-arm tactics—threats and beatings—against workers who did not want to join their unions.

Nevertheless, from the 1950s to the 1970s, unions succeeded in winning more rights for their workers. The eight-hour day had become the standard in American industry. In addition, unions succeeded in achieving new benefits for workers—ones that had been unheard of only a generation earlier. The UAW won cost-of-living adjustments (COLAs) in their multiyear contracts—automatic annual wage increases as the cost of living rose. Also, the union contracts included supplementary unemployment benefits—in addition to government unemployment benefits—that were paid by the employers when workers were laid off from their jobs.

The United Mine Workers led the way in achieving health care benefits for its members. The union built hospitals in the coal regions for its members and their families. Meanwhile, unions had also obtained pensions from employers to supplement social security when workers retired, and workers had the right to vest in their pensions. Vesting meant that after several years on the job, workers not only qualified for pensions, but could also take the pensions with them if they left one employer and went to work somewhere else. They also had the right to retire early and receive pension income. By the 1970s, according to Zieger and Gall, "pensions, health insurance, and the like had become so commonplace that millions of Americans took these hard-won benefits for granted." However, there were still other rights yet to be achieved.

3

Rights for Minorities and Women

In 1963 African Americans who worked at the Ford Motor Company were hired to fill only a small number of jobs. These included low-paying positions as security guards, mail clerks, messengers, and telephone operators. All other positions were closed to them because they were black. According to one critic, African Americans, along with Hispanic workers, were given "the meanest and dirtiest jobs" in the workplace, such as those of janitors and garbage collectors. Ford was not the only place where minority workers faced discrimination. They were barred from entering apprenticeship programs to become trained carpenters, machinists, or electricians. According to one expert, African Americans "had virtually no jobs that involved personal contact with white customers such as retail clerks, bank tellers, airline stewardesses, and cashiers." Employers feared that white customers would not want to deal with them.

FEW AFRICAN AMERICANS HELD HIGH-PAYING FACTORY JOBS BEFORE THE CIVIL RIGHTS ACT WAS PASSED IN 1964. HERE, A BLACK AUTO WORKER INSTALLS ENGINES AT THE FORD MOTOR PLANT IN DETROIT.

Indeed, minorities faced discrimination in every aspect of American life. African-American children were forced to attend separate schools, inferior to those that served white schoolchildren. Black families were required to live in segregated neighborhoods because no one would sell them homes in white neighborhoods. On city transportation, they were told to sit in the back of buses—reserved for blacks only—while whites rode in the front. Throughout the South, Jim Crow laws discriminated against blacks, preventing them from voting and forcing them to drink at separate water fountains, attend separate restaurants, and stay at separate hotels.

During the 1950s African Americans began to protest the unfair treatment they faced across the United States. Led by activists such as Dr. Martin Luther King Jr. and civil rights organizations like the National Association for the Advancement of Colored People (NAACP), they staged massive demonstrations and protest marches. Finally, in the early 1960s, the federal government passed a series of laws to end discrimination.

Civil Rights Act of 1964

In 1964 President Lyndon Johnson signed the Civil Rights Act. Among other things, the new law banned discrimination in the workplace based on race, color, religion, or gender. To enforce the new law, Congress established the Equal Employment Opportunity Commission (EEOC). As a result of the new legislation and lawsuits brought by the NAACP and other civil rights groups, discrimination began to be reduced in the workplace. Gradually, businesses opened up more and more blue collar jobs and management positions to African Americans. Meanwhile, colleges began to open their doors to minority students. As they obtained college degrees and gained admission to graduate school, an increasing number of African Americans and other minorities entered the professions previously closed to them—medicine, law, and accounting.

The Civil Rights Act of 1964 had mentioned "affirmative action" as a method of ending discrimination and creating a balanced workforce. A year later President Johnson signed Executive Order 11246, stating that contractors doing business with the government had to take affirmative action to eliminate discrimination against minorities. Companies conducting business with the federal government realized that they could not win new contracts unless they ended discrimination practices prohibited by the new law. This often meant establishing hiring goals for minorities. In 1967 the law was expanded to eliminate discrimination against women.

Studies have shown that affirmative action increased the number of minority workers and women employed by contractors doing business with the government. That increase was greater than among those businesses not engaged in federal contracts. Nevertheless, affirmative action also created enormous controversy in the workplace. Many white employees claimed their companies were practicing reverse discrimination. That is, they felt that jobs were going to minorities, whether or not they were qualified.

Meanwhile, qualified white employees were facing reverse discrimination and not being hired for the same positions. Supporters of affirmative action claimed that it was making up for "past exclusion" of minorities from positions in the workplace. They argued that in the past white males had benefited from discrimination. White students had filled positions in colleges because they were not open to equally qualified minorities. Whites had received jobs, some of which should have gone to equally qualified minority workers. Opening up new jobs to minorities was not enough, they said. Decades of excluding minorities meant that the workplace would still remain heavily white. In short, there would be no equality unless more jobs were opened up to minority workers.

Critics of affirmative action argued just as strongly that the practice was entirely unfair. As authors Francine

Blau and Anne Winkler point out, these critics argued that "Instead of doing justice, preferential treatment violates rights (the right of an applicant 'to equal consideration,' the right of the [most] competent to an open position, the right of everyone to equal opportunity)." Some African Americans also believed that affirmative action called their qualifications into question. Some people might believe that they had obtained a position in the workplace simply because they were members of a minority group, not because they were actually qualified. As a result, talented African Americans felt that their qualifications would never be fully recognized.

Cases regarding affirmative action eventually came before the U.S. Supreme Court. The justices ruled that affirmative action was necessary to ensure diversity in the workplace. However, an individual's race should only be one factor that an employer considered when filling a position, the Supreme Court justices said. Many other factors—especially the job applicant's qualifications—were essential whenever an employer made a hiring decision. Employers must do far more than simply achieve goals in an effort to hire a specific number of minorities.

Meanwhile, many corporations began to develop affirmative action programs. As one expert on diversity, Deborah Dagit, explained, "Having a more diverse team leads to greater innovation as well as opening the possibilities of different perspectives." As businesses expanded their customer bases, they were selling more and more products to diverse consumers. These businesses recognized the need to have minority employees who could create new products that might appeal to minority consumers and develop strong customer relationships with them.

While minority employees made huge gains in the workplace, they continued to face some discrimination. In 1996, Wayne Elliot, an African American, went to work at a warehouse owned by Lockheed Martin Corporation in

Marietta, Georgia. At the huge aircraft plant, Elliot said that he saw racist statements on the walls of bathrooms. His supervisor referred to him as "boy," a negative term often used in the past by whites in the South to refer to African-American men. When Elliot and other black workers at the plant protested, a rope in the shape of a hangman's noose was put on his desk. The noose recalled the treatment of blacks accused of violent crimes in the South. They were routinely lynched by white mobs instead of receiving a fair trial.

According to *Business Week*, which conducted studies in 2001, racial incidents were still occurring in the workplace. Companies such as Texaco, the giant oil company, and Boeing, the large aircraft manufacturer, were being charged with racism by employees. Indeed, approximately nine thousand racial incidents were brought to the attention of the EEOC between 1990 and 2001. Some of these were cases like Wayne Elliot's, such as a complaint by construction workers at Northwest Airlines.

In 2000 Coca-Cola lost a class action suit brought by employees who charged the giant soft-drink maker with racial discrimination. In 2003 another class action suit was brought against Coca-Cola for racial discrimination. African-American employees charged the company with "creating a hostile, intimidating, offensive and abusive workplace environment for its African-American employees." They said that supervisors had "allowed white employees to use racial slurs and threats and to physically abuse minority employees."

In 2004 John Deere—the farm- and lawn-equipment maker—was forced to recruit minority and women dealers. This occurred after a lawsuit charged that none of its dealers were women or members of minority groups. In 2005 Abercrombie & Fitch, the large retail chain, was forced to pay $40 million to African-American, Latino, and Asian-American female employees and those who

41

Minority-Owned Businesses

Following the passage of the Civil Rights Act of 1964, the federal government awarded a substantial number of contracts to minority-owned businesses. As a result, they could compete on an equal footing with white-owned companies, which had done business in Washington, D.C., for many years. State and city governments followed the same practice, providing new business that helped minority-owned companies achieve success. But abuses gradually appeared in the system. One example occurred in Shreveport, Louisiana. A councilman accused white contractors of using "black faces as fronts" for their businesses. The *Shreveport Times* reported that

> **it's not unheard of that a minority-owned business would receive a city-related contract and then pass . . . [the] business to a white-owned contractor. In the case of the city's effort to privatize its water billing operation, minority-owned Port Cities Utilities was awarded the contract, yet the actual meter-reading work was turned over to a white-owned business, Northwest Louisiana Services.**

But there were only a small number of businesses that violated the Civil Rights Act compared with those who played by the rules and followed the law.

applied for jobs. They accused the company of practicing racial discrimination when hiring employees.

Women in the Workplace

In the 1960s airlines traditionally did not hire married women as flight attendants. United Airlines, for example, said this decision had been made because men married to women flight attendants were unhappy when their wives had to travel away from home and work long hours. Nevertheless, airlines did not apply the same rule to male employees, such as pilots. The women at United sued the airline for unfair treatment. In its 1977 ruling in the case of *United Airlines, Inc.* v. *McDonald*, the Supreme Court said that the women were entitled to reinstatement and back pay. Married women were no longer excluded from the ranks of flight attendants.

In the first half of the twentieth century, women who tried to enter the workplace faced discrimination. Some careers, such as medicine, law, and university professorships, were almost entirely closed to them. Women were also barred from apprenticeship programs where they could learn to be electricians or carpenters, or do other skilled labor. Men did not want to lose these jobs to women. In addition, they believed that women were not as capable of doing them as men.

While women were encouraged to work in factories, very few of them ever became supervisors. They were usually paid less than men for the same work. In 1960 white women earned only about half of what white men made, and minority women were paid even less. Women also encountered sexual harassment on the job—including lewd remarks from male workers and requests for sexual favors from managers.

The Civil Rights Act of 1964 not only outlawed dis-

IN POST–WORLD WAR II AMERICA, STEWARDESSES WERE SEEN AS
DECORATIVE OBJECTS, NOT THE HARD WORKERS THEY WERE, AS
SHOWN IN THE WAY THEY ARE POSED IN THIS 1956 ADVERTISEMENT
FOR A BOEING JETLINER.

crimination against minorities, but also against women in
the workplace. A year earlier Congress had passed the
Equal Pay Act, requiring that men and women who did
substantially the same work should receive the same pay.

As a result of this legislation, changes began to occur for women seeking jobs. Professional schools began to open their doors to women who wanted to become lawyers or doctors. More women embarked on careers in medicine and law. Women also began to fill positions in police and fire departments that had been closed to them in the past. In addition, women's pay began to increase, and by 1980 they were making far more than they had twenty years earlier.

Although women achieved substantial progress in the workplace, they discovered that achieving equal rights with men would not be fully accomplished by new laws alone.

For example, in 1994 there were twelve times as many male professors as female professors in the School of Sciences at the Massachusetts Institute of Technology (MIT), located in Boston. Although a woman, Susan Hockfield, was appointed president of the university, negative attitudes toward women in academia still continue. President Lawrence Summers of Harvard University claimed in a speech delivered in 2005 that fewer women than men went into math and science because of inborn differences between females and males. He later resigned, at least in part because of his remarks, and was replaced by a female president—Dr. Drew Faust.

According to author Raymond Gregory, men often believe that women have a dual role that makes it difficult for them to assume top-level positions in any organization. They must divide their time between working and raising children. As a result, some men believe women cannot totally commit themselves to a job in the way that men who have wives at home can. Indeed, Gregory adds, many employers regard the "ideal worker" as one who is totally committed to the job with little time left for family responsibilities. Women, in the eyes of these employers, don't fit into this employee model.

Women at law firms have faced the same type of discrimination as the professors at MIT. In 1999 only one major New York City firm had a woman as its managing partner, or head. While more than 40 percent of all lawyers at major firms were women, only 12 percent had become partners—that is, those who were paid the highest salaries and had ownership in the firm. According to one study, female lawyers had often taken time off to have children. When they returned, Gregory pointed out, they said they "were denied more coveted work and case assignments" that would help them progress to partnership. "Moreover, an expectation seemed to form in the firm that now that they were mothers they would withdraw from the partnership track. . . . Women, moreover, were often categorized as 'outsiders' and perceived to be less committed to the firm. Sex stereotyping and the treatment of women as a category rather than as individuals provided serious obstacles to advancement."

Even those women who tried to break out of the stereotype faced severe problems. Most women were considered to be too soft—not assertive enough to be partners. Those who exhibited assertiveness, however, were often called too tough and too masculine by their male colleagues. By the twenty-first century this situation had gradually changed. More women were becoming partners in law firms. But in many organizations, women still faced a glass ceiling. There seemed to be a limit as to how far they could climb up the career ladder.

According to Catalyst, a nonprofit feminist research organization, approximately half of all management positions were filled by women in 2006. Yet, fewer than 2 percent of chief executive officers at America's largest companies were female. In addition, women who have filled elective political office are relatively few in number compared to other nations of the world. In fact, the United

States ranks fifty-eighth among the world's nations when it comes to the number of females who fill political leadership roles. No woman, for example, has ever been elected president of the United States. However, Congresswoman Nancy Pelosi became the first female Speaker of the House of Representatives in 2007.

In terms of pay women have made significant strides. However, their paychecks still amount to only 75 to 85 percent of men's for similar work. As author Lawrence Reed wrote, "Because women experience more interruptions in their working careers than do men—usually because of marriage or childbearing—the wages they can command in the market are slightly discounted. This is not unfair; indeed, it is perfectly rational economic behavior on the part of employers concerned about their bottom lines." But Reed forgets about those women who do not take time off but still receive less pay than men.

Unfairness may be at play, at least in some organizations. At Morgan Stanley, a large financial services firm, women sued because of discrimination in terms of pay and promotion. They were not paid as much as men for comparable work, nor were they treated equally when it came to promotions. In 2004 the EEOC announced that these women would collectively receive $54 million to settle the case. A similar case was brought against Home Depot during the 1990s. In this case women were awarded $87.5 million.

Sexual Harassment

In addition to claims of discrimination, women have also faced sexual harassment on the job. This includes sexual advances, requests for sexual favors, and verbal or physical abuse. Most organizations have developed policies expressly prohibiting sexual harassment. Courts have ruled that harassment is a form of discrimination because women face this problem from male supervisors and coworkers simply because they are female. Sometimes a female worker finds herself in a position of being pressured into accepting a supervisor's sexual advances out of fear of losing her job. In the 1980s, Mechelle Vinson sued the Meritor Savings Bank, where she claimed that she had been sexually harassed by her supervisor, Sidney Taylor. According to Vinson, Taylor wanted to initiate a sexual affair with her. At first, Vinson said nothing, but when she protested, she was fired on the grounds that she had taken too much sick leave.

In its ruling on the case in 1984, the U.S. Supreme Court stated,

Sexual harassment which creates a hostile or offensive environment for one sex is every bit the arbitrary barrier to sexual equality at the workplace that racial harassment is to racial equality. Surely, a requirement that a man or woman run a gauntlet of sexual abuse in return for the privilege of being allowed to work and make a living can be as demeaning and disconcerting as the harshest of racial epithets.

Nevertheless, sexual harassment often creates serious problems not only for female employees but for their employers as well. According to the Civil Rights Act of 1991, women could sue an employer for punitive damages—punishing an employer who permitted sexual harassment to occur. *Forbes* magazine pointed out that lawsuits began to grow to millions of dollars as women sued their employers over sexual harassment. These claims not only involved an employer's sexual advances, but an environment that seemed hostile to women. A hostile environment was one in which male employees told sexual jokes or made sexual remarks about women.

"Men are retreating to the safety of their offices, avoiding private contact with female co-workers and carefully censoring their speech," according to the conservative *National Review* magazine. But the National Association of Working Women countered, "No one has ever called our hotline to say, 'My manager calls me Honey or says I looked nice today.' People call to say, 'So and so is groping me, came to my hotel room. . . .'"

While many women may have legitimate claims of harassment, others may not. Thus, an important workers' right can easily be abused.

4
Workers' Benefits and the Decline of the Unions

The struggle for workers' rights has been fought on many battlegrounds. Among these was the Point Blank Body Armor factory in Oakland Park, Florida. In 2002 a group of workers at the plant, led by Sadius Isma—an immigrant from Haiti—asked their employer if they could form a union. According to Isma, the manager said that unions at the plant were illegal. The workers were prevented by the company from returning to their jobs, and Isma was fired. Although the National Labor Relations Board intervened, the company continued to battle in court against unionization. As author David Moberg wrote, Isma's experience is not unusual: "When workers throughout the United States try to organize unions, they nearly always face systematic employer opposition, both legal and illegal, that intimidates many union-friendly workers, encourages anti-union hostility from other employers and creates a political climate that makes union organizing extremely difficult."

Workers' Rights Affected by the Decline of Unions

Over the past thirty years, union membership dropped drastically from a high of 35 percent of workers in 1945 to about 12 percent today. This has had a major impact on workers' rights. In part, the decline of the unions has occurred because of the drop in manufacturing in the United States. Hundreds of thousands of union members who worked in these industries lost their jobs. Many companies moved their plants to other parts of the world, such as Central America and Asia. In these areas, wages are much lower, so the cost of doing business is far less. To compete in the global marketplace, companies have been forced to cut costs. This is the only way that they can match the prices of goods made in other countries that are shipped to the United States.

Other companies that remained in the United States have threatened to move their operations overseas if employees joined a union. This has frightened many workers into remaining nonunion employees. While manufacturing jobs declined, the number of companies in service industries—like hotels and restaurants—and in high-tech, computer-related fields, increased enormously. These businesses have been traditionally nonunion. A tremendous increase has also occurred in the number of small companies, which employ few workers—another area that has traditionally remained nonunion.

Meanwhile, the power of the NLRB has weakened. Beginning in the 1980s, Republican presidents like Ronald Reagan appointed pro-business members to the NLRB. They were far more willing to support employers who tried to resist unionization. Indeed, the action taken by the NLRB at Point Blank Body Armor was unusual. Many states also adopted right-to-work laws, which protected workers who did not want to join unions.

UNION MEMBERSHIP IS NOW LOWER THAN IT HAS BEEN IN A
HUNDRED YEARS, IN MANY CASES BECAUSE OF GOVERNMENT ACTION.
ON OCTOBER 5, 2006, NURSES IN DOWNTOWN LOS ANGELES
PROTESTED A RULING BY THE NATIONAL LABOR RELATIONS BOARD
THAT WOULD PREVENT NURSE SUPERVISORS FROM BELONGING TO
A UNION.

Retiree Medical Benefits

The decline of the unions has been a major factor affecting
workers' benefits. For example, during the mid-twentieth
century, unions began pressuring large employers to provide their workers with retiree medical insurance. This

insurance covered medical costs not paid by Medicare. Passed by Congress in 1965 during the administration of President Lyndon Johnson, Medicare provides health care benefits for retired workers age sixty-five and older.

At first the cost of retiree medical insurance was low. But over the past few decades, health care costs have skyrocketed. As a result, many companies have begun to drop retiree medical insurance from their benefit package. This has become easier because of the weakening influence of

SENIORS ARE HIT HARD BY CUTS IN MEDICAL INSURANCE. IN 1998, A GROUP OF SENIORS RALLIED IN NEW YORK TO DEMAND NATIONAL HEALTH INSURANCE, A DEMAND THAT HASN'T BEEN MET.

the labor unions. In 1988, for example, two-thirds of large companies employing more than two hundred workers provided their employees with retiree medical benefits. By the early twenty-first century, this number had dropped to approximately one-third of all large firms. With the number of retirees growing each year, many companies realized that the expense of health insurance was becoming too much for them to afford and still make reasonable profits.

Without retiree health benefits, many workers who thought about taking early retirement at age fifty-five or sixty have been forced to wait until they are covered by Medicare at age sixty-five. Unfortunately, Medicare does not cover all health care expenses. Retirees must also carry additional insurance to pick up the remaining costs. These policies may cost more than many retirees can afford.

Health Benefits for Workers

Workers are not only concerned about retiree health benefits, but also about health care packages that cover them and their families while they are still working. Health benefits were part of agreements won by unions during the twentieth century. Today a majority of workers receive some type of health insurance from their employers. However, as the costs of health care have increased, insurance coverage has changed. In the 1980s, when expenses were lower, large employers often paid for the complete cost of health insurance. More recently, health insurance premiums have been increasing at 15 percent or more per year, costing more than six thousand dollars per employee.

As a result, over the past few decades most companies have required their workers to pay for a larger and larger share of health insurance premiums. Many employers require workers to pick up as much as half of monthly health insurance costs to cover themselves and their families. The insurance may also provide less coverage than in the past. For example, employees may have larger deductibles—money they have to pay—for medical procedures.

Many small companies cannot afford to provide any form of health insurance for their employees. Insurance rates are lower for large firms with many employees. Higher rates for smaller organizations often make health insurance unaffordable. Health care costs are also increasing faster for small companies than for larger firms. In addition, large companies may offer insurance only to those employees who work full time. They may also require a waiting period of at least three months after an employee has been hired before he or she can qualify for insurance. A recent survey of workers in Milwaukee, Wisconsin, for instance, found that large employers, such as McDonald's, did not provide health insurance for many of its restaurant workers. Instead, they were forced to rely on the BadgerCare program, which provides health care to low-income families.

In Massachusetts, uninsured workers rely on Medicaid for health care. This program, which is funded by state and federal tax money, provides care for low-income people. A 2006 survey found that many of these residents held low-wage and part-time jobs at companies like Burger King, Wendy's, Wal-Mart stores, and Stop & Shop, a large chain of supermarkets. In 2006 Massachusetts became the first state to require everyone who can afford health insurance to buy it. Low-income people who cannot afford insurance will be covered by health insurance policies with no premiums.

Nationwide, only about half of employees earning less than ten dollars an hour have health insurance from their employers. During the first part of the twenty-first century, Americans without health insurance increased by 5 million people. In fact, more than 36 million workers lack any kind of health insurance coverage from their employers.

Several million make enough money to buy their own insurance. Approximately 16 million are covered by members of their family who receive health insurance where they work. But a total of 13 million workers are completely uninsured.

Most of the uninsured cannot afford to purchase health insurance for themselves and their families. A survey in Connecticut revealed that about 66 percent of the uninsured work for small companies. The majority are under age forty, unmarried, and more likely to be members of minority groups. They also made low incomes—under $30,000 per year.

The cost of paying for uninsured Americans has also proven to be very heavy. In Milwaukee, for example, the estimated cost of providing health care to uninsured workers and their families was over $12 million in 2006. In 2005 Massachusetts spent an estimated $213 million to insure 160,000 employees and their families covered by Medicaid.

In the 1990s political leaders in Washington proposed a system of government-run universal health care coverage to insure those who are currently uninsured. Opponents of government-sponsored health insurance claim that it would reduce the quality of health care, pointing to other government health care systems in England and Canada. In addition, they argue that a government program will involve a large bureaucracy that would slow down the delivery of health care and lead to long waiting lines for operations and other types of medical procedures. Finally, they believe that if the poor, with chronic health problems, have insurance, they will use the health care system and go to doctors far too often—increasing the burden on American medical facilities and American taxpayers.

Not only do many employees in the United States lack health insurance, they may also work without any paid sick leave. According to the Institute for Women's Policy

The Cost of Medical Care

Some hospitals believe that preventive care—visits to the doctor—for the poor with chronic health problems is the best way to save money. Hospitals have realized this after stepping in to provide care at almost no cost to the working poor who have no health insurance. One of these workers was Dee Dee Dodd, who lives in Austin, Texas. Dodd suffers from diabetes, which requires her to take insulin. Since she could not afford insurance, Dodd tried to take care of herself instead of making regular visits to a doctor to monitor her diabetes. This approach was unsuccessful, however, and each month Dodd had to be rushed to the emergency room of Seton Hospital in Austin.

After repeated trips, her medicals bills had reached almost $200,000, which she could not pay. Seton finally decided that it was much cheaper to offer Dodd free preventive care so she could visit a doctor regularly. Then, the doctor could monitor her diabetes and take action before her disease grew out of control. As a result, her medical bills have been reduced by 50 percent.

Seton offers similar care to others whose income falls below the U.S. poverty line—$13,200 per year for a two-person family. Hospital specialists are assigned to patients being helped under the program. Their responsibility is to monitor each patient's condition to ensure that it does not become a medical emergency. Other hospitals across the United States are adopting a similar approach. But, this effort is only reaching a small number of the working poor who are uninsured. According to Karen Davis of the Commonwealth Fund, a foundation with broad experience in health care, "All these local efforts are commendable, but they are like sticking fingers in the dikes."

Research, an estimated 60 million workers do not receive paid sick leave. As many as 89 million workers receive less than seven paid sick days annually. Some businesses argue that they cannot afford to pay an employee to stay at home and simultaneously lose his or her productive work. In addition, an employer may have to hire a temporary employee to replace the worker who is out on sick leave. A 2003 survey by *USA Today* revealed that absenteeism by employees who are not really sick is "epidemic."

Although there are problems providing sick leave, there are also benefits. Studies show that a worker with a bad cold or the flu who does not come into the workplace lessens the chance of infecting other employees, who may then be forced to take sick leave. In addition, the health of workers who stay at home generally improves more rapidly so they can return to work sooner, fully recovered.

Health Benefits for Gay and Lesbian Workers

In 1992, Levi Strauss & Co., the giant clothing maker headquartered in San Francisco, became the first company to offer health benefits to the partners of employees who formed same-sex couples. This was a groundbreaking development at a time when most homosexual workers were afraid to admit that they were gay or lesbian. They feared that coworkers would not accept their homosexuality. Currently, over 50 percent of Fortune 500 corporations offer these benefits to same-sex domestic partners. They also provide these benefits to heterosexual couples who live together outside of marriage. As a result, workers and their partners do not have to bear the financial expense of paying for health insurance themselves. Domestic partners are defined as couples who have been living together for at least six months, depend on each other for financial expenses, are not bound together by marriage, and share checking accounts, mortgage payments, and other housing expenses.

Laws do not require employers to provide health insurance benefits. And many of them have been criticized for offering these benefits to gay and lesbian couples. In 2000, for example, the Family Research Council issued a sharply worded statement against Ford, Chrysler, and General Motors for providing these benefits. The council said that it supports the "traditional family unit" of a heterosexual couple with children. Census statistics released in 2006, however, show that only a minority of families in the United States are so-called traditional units.

Women and the Family and Medical Leave Act

For many years, similar attitudes were encountered by women who had to care for a sick family member or a newborn child. Routinely, women who left the workplace to give birth to a child found that there was no job for them when they tried to return to work at their organization. In 1993 Congress changed this situation with the passage of the Family and Medical Leave Act (FMLA). Under the terms of the act, employees are permitted to take up to twelve weeks of unpaid leave to care for a baby, a sick child, or other family members. Employers with fifty or more employees must provide this benefit to workers who have been employed at the organization for twelve months. After this period, the worker must be offered a job comparable to the one that she held before leaving her employment. Some organizations provide employees with paid leave. Many workers are also permitted under the terms of the act to leave work for short periods during the day due to an illness that requires regular treatment, such as cancer.

As a result of the act, Patti Phillips was permitted by

Discrimination and Homosexual Employees

More than two thousand companies have issued policies prohibiting discrimination in hiring homosexual employees. Eleven states have also passed laws outlawing discrimination against homosexual workers. Nevertheless, many homosexuals still face stiff prejudice that prevents them from being hired. In Georgia, Robin Shahar, a recent law school graduate, had obtained a job with a law firm after receiving her degree from Emory Law School in Atlanta, Georgia. However, the head of the firm learned that Shahar was a lesbian who was in a relationship with another woman whom she planned to marry. As a result, the offer to work at the firm was withdrawn. As the partner in charge of the firm explained, "inaction on my part would constitute tacit approval of this . . . marriage and jeopardize the proper functioning of this office." Since Georgia has no law preventing discrimination against homosexual workers, Shahar could not win a lawsuit.

In Massachusetts, however, Michael Salvi faced a similar situation and did sue his employer. Salvi had been employed as a corrections officer in Suffolk County since 1994. Somehow, coworkers discovered that Salvi was gay and began to make derogatory remarks about him. At first, Salvi tried to put up with the treatment from his coworkers. But he began suffering from depression. When he went to his superiors, they demoted him. Eventually, Salvi was advised by his doctor to quit because he had developed a heart condition. Salvi sued the sheriff's office that employed him as a corrections officer. A jury decided that he had been a victim of sexual harassment and awarded him a settlement of about $624,000.

The U.S. Congress has been considering the Employment Nondiscrimination Act (ENDA), which would prohibit discrimination against workers based on their sexual orientation. Those lawmakers who oppose the legislation have argued that it protects certain workers based only "on certain behaviors [that can be changed] rather than an immutable trait." According to the American Psychological Association (APA), "most psychologists do not consider sexual orientation for most people to be a conscious choice that can be voluntarily changed." Those who oppose the ENDA have also stated that it requires coworkers to accept colleagues whose "behavior they find objectionable." That is, some workers believe that gay males might be guilty of molesting children. However, the APA has pointed out that most sexual abuse is committed by heterosexual males. In addition, the APA emphasizes that it "is a fundamental value . . . that all working people have a right to be judged by the quality of their work performance and not by completely unrelated factors."

Nevertheless, in a recent survey of employers nationwide, over 25 percent said they would not hire—and almost 20 percent said they would fire—any employees of either sex who admitted that they were homosexuals.

her employer to spend many days in the hospital with her daughter, Stephanie, who eventually died of bone cancer. In Connecticut, a lawyer took twelve weeks of unpaid leave after giving birth to her first child. Her employer held open the lawyer's position after the birth of her child, and she returned to work three months later.

Nevertheless, the FMLA has created heated controversies. In small companies, the loss of even a single employee for twelve weeks can be a burden on an employer. The organization may need to find a temporary replacement, which can be extremely difficult. If no replacement can be found, other employees must take over the duties of the worker who is out on leave. Critics of the law, like the U.S. Chamber of Commerce, also claim that employees often use it to take time off from work for minor illnesses—like a cold or a headache. A study by the Employment Policy Foundation found that the act "cost employers $21 billion in 2004." Nevertheless, Linda Meric of the National Association of Working Women in Milwaukee, Wisconsin, contends, "When workers aren't covered by the FMLA, they frequently lose their jobs when they have to take off to care for their own medical condition or a family member. They lose their income and have to go on public assistance. People shouldn't have to choose between a healthy family and a paycheck."

The rights provided under the FMLA apply to male as well as female workers. Nevertheless, women more often than men take extended leaves to care for newborn children or sick family members.

Pregnancy Discrimination Act

FMLA is considered an extension of an earlier law designed to protect pregnant women against discrimination—the Pregnancy Discrimination Act of 1978. According to the law, pregnant women cannot be treated any differently in the workplace than other employees. The law, an amendment to the Civil Rights Act of 1964, was passed after court decisions stating that the Civil Rights Act did not apply to pregnant women.

Caroline Sanford was employed by the Yenkin-Majestic Paint Corporation in Ohio. Sanford had secretarial duties, as well as responsibility for writing technical reports including chemical information about the company's paint products. After working at the company for several months, Sanford told her supervisor that she was pregnant. Soon afterward, her department was eliminated. Although another job existed in the company for someone with her experience, it was not offered to her. Instead, Sanford was fired. Sanford took her case to the Equal Employment Opportunity Commission (EEOC), which sued the paint company under the Pregnancy Discrimination Act. Sanford won her case.

Although the Pregnancy Discrimination Act protects female employees, it can also create serious problems for employers. Suppose a supervisor has been displeased with an employee's work. He has spoken to her in the past, but her job efficiency has not improved. The supervisor has decided to fire the employee, but before he acts she comes into his office and announces that she is pregnant. If the supervisor fires the female employee at this point, she can sue the organization for discrimination.

The Pregnancy Discrimination Act not only protects women from being fired if they become pregnant, but also from losing any pay because of their pregnancy. Employers are also prohibited from refusing to hire pregnant women. In 2004 almost three-quarters of women with children were employed. That year the EEOC handled more than 4,500 cases involving the Pregnancy Discrimination Act. As many employers learned, pregnant women must be treated just like any other employee.

5
Rights of Disabled and Aging Workers

Michael Gravitt's eyesight has been so bad since childhood that he is considered legally blind. As a child, he couldn't participate in sports or most of the other activities that his friends enjoyed. "The computer was really my only outlet as a child," he recalled. "It really fascinated me and by the time I was eleven or twelve years old, I was writing simple programs." Gravitt attended college and graduated in 1997 with a business degree, specializing in management information systems. Eventually, he found a job with Bayer Corporation, the giant pharmaceuticals company. "Typically, for someone in my position," he said, "the greatest challenge is getting a job. Finding an environment that is open-minded to . . . diversity can be a struggle." But Bayer provided just the right environment for someone like Gravitt, who is disabled. They put special software on his computer that enlarges the type so he can see it easily. For those employees who are completely blind, "All Web sites must be able to work with speech software," Gravitt explained.

Americans with Disabilities Act

Employees like Michael Gravitt receive legal protection under the 1990 Americans with Disabilities Act (ADA). According to the act, organizations with fifteen or more employees cannot discriminate against disabled workers who have "a physical or mental impairment that sub-

IN 1990, PRESIDENT GEORGE H. W. BUSH SIGNED THE AMERICANS WITH DISABILITIES ACT INTO LAW.

stantially limits one or more major life activities." There are 50 million Americans with disabilities. These might be workers who are legally blind like Gravitt, deaf, unable to walk, or suffering from an illness like severe diabetes. Discrimination is prohibited in the hiring of employees. Anyone who has all the qualifications—education and experience—for performing a job cannot be turned down for a position simply because of a disability. These workers also cannot be required to take a medical examination until after they have been offered a position, and only if all other employees are required to submit to the same exams. For qualified employees with disabilities, employers must provide "reasonable accommodations" that will enable them to perform effectively. These accommodations may take the form of special software on their computers, for example, or speech software. Office buildings should have ramps so workers can roll their wheelchairs up to the main doors. Equal benefits must also be provided for employees. For example, if an employer has a lunch room or lounge on the second floor that is only accessible by stairs, an elevator must be installed in the building for employees in wheelchairs, or a similar lounge must be created on the first floor.

The only limitation on these accommodations is "undue hardship" on the employer. This means that the cost would be too high for the employer to pay. However, the government provides financial assistance, such as business tax deductions, to employers who provide these accommodations. Under the ADA, employers are also expected to make work schedules more flexible for disabled workers who need them. For instance, a worker who has severe diabetes may be required to go for dialysis on a regular basis during the day to purify his or her blood. As a result, he or she might need to be given time off and be permitted to make up the hours by staying later in the evening.

Settlements under the ADA

The EEOC has the major responsibility for enforcing the ADA. Since the act was passed, the commission has won an estimated $600 million for almost 40,000 workers with disabilities. Some of the cases that the EEOC has won include that of a blind worker who was not permitted to hold a customer service job for which he was otherwise qualified, and a mentally challenged restaurant worker fired by a supervisor who said that he did not want "people like that" working for him. In 2004, DaimlerChrysler, the automaker, was required to pay $4.6 million to Melinda Young, a physically disabled employee, who claimed that the company had refused to offer her certain positions because of her disability. According to her lawyer, Richard Darst, "The jury intended to send a message to corporations that they cannot discriminate against someone because they are disabled."

Nevertheless, many disabled workers run into serious obstacles, whether they are looking for a new position from their employer or even trying to convince an organization to hire them. Although the ADA prohibits discrimination, illegal hiring practices continue to exist in the workplace, and disabled workers are often denied jobs. According to a 2004 study conducted by Cornell University, only about 38 percent of disabled adult workers are currently employed. Some unemployed workers with disabilities are collecting money from social security. Approximately 8 million workers collect Social Security Disability Income (SSDI). But this amounts to an average of only $894 monthly. Nevertheless, individuals are forced to give up part of this income if they are making over $830 a month for a period of nine months. "That's a whale of a disincentive to work," says Doug Kruse of Rutgers University.

Reasonable Accommodations

Many organizations believe that providing "reasonable accommodations" for the disabled will be very expensive. However, Rutgers University found in a 2003 study that the cost of these accommodations is usually quite low. The average cost is lower than five hundred dollars per employee. Many employers found that no changes in their work environment were necessary to accommodate the disabled employees. Other employers believe, without even interviewing disabled applicants, that they would probably lack the skills to do the job.

Even after disabled workers are hired, they often face discrimination from employers. Carolyn Pisani went to work for Home Depot in South Setauket, Long Island, in 1999. Pisani's intelligence level, as measured by an IQ test, was only 60, putting her below average. She was assigned a job coach, who worked for the New York State Education Department, to help her learn her job responsibilities. There are over 100,000 such coaches working with disabled workers in the United States. Pisani was responsible for helping customers who were shopping for various types of electrical merchandise, such as home lighting. After four months on the job, Pisani was criticized by her boss for not coming to work on two days. She claimed that she had received a telephone call from someone who said he worked for Home Depot telling her to remain at home. As a result of missing the workdays, Pisani was given a negative employment report and fired.

"She was devastated," her lawyer Susan Slavin said. "This job meant a great deal to her. She had pride in her work." Although Home Depot said that it was justified in firing Pisani, the store decided to pay her $75,000 to avoid going to court. Since that time, she has found jobs with other employers.

In March 2005 a much higher settlement was received by an employee at Wal-Mart, the huge discount chain store. He was a pharmacist with cerebral palsy—brain damage that affects muscle coordination—who said that managers had not permitted him to work in the pharmacy. They told him that he was not "fit for the pharmacy job." Instead, he was ordered to work outside the store collecting shopping carts. This was a violation of the ADA. The pharmacist sued Wal-Mart, collecting more than $7.5 million.

In some cases, however, the interpretation of the ADA may not be so clear. In 2002, for example, the U.S. Supreme Court heard the case of *U.S. Airways* v. *Barnett*. Barnett was a disabled cargo handler who had suffered a back injury while working for the large airline. Therefore, he asked his supervisor to find a less physically demanding position for him. Barnett was eventually moved to the mailroom. Nevertheless, his position did not remain permanent. U.S. Airways permitted employees with more seniority—longer employment—to apply for the position. One of these workers who was not disabled received the job, and Barnett was fired. He sued U.S. Airways for discrimination under the ADA.

In a 5 to 4 decision the U.S. Supreme Court decided that Barnett was not covered by the ADA. Justice Stephen Breyer delivered the majority opinion for the court. He said that there was a conflict between

the interests of a disabled worker who seeks assignment to a particular position as a "reasonable accommodation" . . . and the interests of other workers with superior rights to bid for the job under an employer's seniority system. . . . In our view, the seniority system will prevail. . . . As we interpret the statute (ADA), to show that a requested

accommodation conflicts with the rules of a seniority system is ordinarily to show that the accommodation is not "reasonable."

Among the judges who disagreed was Justice David Souter, who said, "Nothing in the ADA insulates [protects] seniority rules from the 'reasonable accommodation' requirement." Looking at the discussions in Congress when the ADA was passed, Souter said that seniority systems "should not amount to more than 'a factor'" when considering reasonable accommodations.

In another case, *Toyota Motor Manufacturing, Kentucky, Inc., Petitioner v. Ella Williams*, the Supreme Court decided by a 9 to 0 vote that the ADA did not protect an employee in a Toyota automobile plant. Ella Williams went to work at the plant, located in Georgetown, Kentucky, in 1990. Williams was employed on an assembly line making automobile engines. After working on the line, she developed carpal tunnel syndrome in her arms and wrists. This disability, which includes severe muscle pains, afflicts many workers who do repetitive work with their hands and arms. As a result of her disability, she was given a new job as an inspector examining the paint job on each new car produced at the plant. Part of this job involved applying oil to each car with a sponge. To perform this job, Williams had to keep her arms parallel with her shoulders for lengthy periods each day. As a result, she again developed carpal tunnel syndrome. When Williams requested another job, she was turned down by her supervisor and advised by her doctor to reduce her working hours. Eventually, Toyota fired her for not coming to work.

Williams sued Toyota, saying that she faced discrimination because of her disability. Under the ADA, a disability is defined as a condition that restricts a "major life activity." These activities include such things as walking, seeing, hearing, learning, and working. Nevertheless, the

Supreme Court ruled that Williams was not disabled simply because she could not perform the job of applying oil to a freshly painted car. Justice Sandra Day O'Connor said that this type of work "is not an important part of most people's daily lives. Household chores, bathing, and brushing one's teeth, in contrast, are among the types of manual tasks of central importance to people's daily lives."

Rights of Aging Workers

The laws relating to disabled workers are not the only ones open to controversy; similar debates occur over laws concerning aging workers.

In 1989 Ron Harper opened an Allstate insurance agency in Thomson, Georgia. Harper had previously been employed in the supermarket industry, working his way up from a bagger to a district manager responsible for more than a dozen stores. But the insurance business seemed to offer a better income, which Harper needed to support his wife and two children. After going through the Allstate training program and receiving a territory to cover, Harper was ready to become an insurance agent. Over the next ten years, he built up a successful business. He also received benefits for himself and his family and qualified for a generous pension when he retired. Then, in November 1999, when Harper was in his late forties, something unexpected happened to him and 6,200 other agents at Allstate. He was told that the company was changing his position to the job of an independent contractor. As a result, he was going to lose all his benefits and his pension. If Harper tried to protest and sue the company, he would no longer be permitted to sell Allstate insurance. "I read that thing, and honest to God, I felt nauseous," Harper recalled.

Although Harper signed an agreement saying that he accepted the new conditions of his employment, he turned around and sued the company. Harper and the other agents who joined him in the suit charged that Allstate was guilty of age discrimination. In 1967 Congress passed the Age Discrimination in Employment Act (ADEA). The law bans discrimination against employees age forty and over. The law applies to companies employing twenty employees or more. It specifically states that these organizations cannot discriminate against workers because of their age in areas such as hiring, giving promotions to employees or increasing their salaries, denying them benefits, or firing them.

In August 2003 the EEOC delivered a ruling on the Allstate case. The commission determined that 6,200 agents like Ron Harper, who had been forced to become independent contractors, had been victims of age discrimination. Allstate had violated the ADEA. "There was no discrimination," claimed a lawyer for Allstate. "We reorganized our agency force for a lot of very good business reasons." The company eliminated many administrative jobs as well as those held by agents, saving $600 million. According to the company, these savings enabled Allstate to compete in the marketplace with other insurance companies, like Geico, which sold insurance to customers over the telephone and the Internet without relying on sales agents.

However, agents at Allstate claimed that part of the reason they had been singled out was age discrimination. As one agent described, "We used to hear it in meetings all the time: 'We have these young people and they really go out and work.' They said older workers just want to sit on their policies [insurance that was already sold to customers] and collect commissions."

Types of Age Discrimination

Age discrimination may come in two forms in the workplace. *Disparate treatment* occurs when employers clearly state that they would like to eliminate older workers in favor of younger ones. This is illegal under the ADEA. An employer may not state this attitude directly to an older employee. However, older workers may hear statements from supervisors, such as, "the department only seems to employ gray-haired people," or, "we need more flexible employees here who can adapt to change." Nevertheless, this type of discrimination may be difficult for older workers to prove. For example, a supervisor may make a statement about "too many gray-haired employees in the department" because he is referring to himself and planning to take early retirement, not because of age discrimination.

Another type of age discrimination is called *disparate impact*. This is an employment policy that does not arise out of discrimination against older workers but still impacts them more than younger ones. In California, for example, a company decided to save money on salaries. As a result, it fired many of the highest-paid employees and recruited new workers at lower salaries to do the same jobs. This had a direct impact on workers over forty because they had been employed by the company for many years and earned the highest salaries. However, the California court ruled that the company had a legal right to make this decision. It was entitled to cut costs to compete in the marketplace. Although the decision affected older workers more than younger ones, this was not the reason that the company made it.

In 2005 the U.S. Supreme Court ruled that employees could now bring lawsuits based on disparate impact. The case, *Smith v. City of Jackson*, involved police officers in Jackson, Mississippi. They brought a lawsuit against the city because it had given raises to officers who had served on the police force for fewer than five years without raising the salaries of officers with longer service. The older officers accused the city of age discrimination. City officials said they decided to make the salaries of younger officers competitive with other police departments in the area. This was the only way that they could recruit and hold on to young officers.

The Supreme Court ruled that under the ADEA, older employees could sue for age discrimination if an employer's decision has a greater impact on them than upon other workers. It makes no difference whether or not that was the intent of the decision. Nevertheless, the court also stated that the "impact on older workers need only be justified by 'reasonable' non-age factors." The Supreme Court said that the decision by Jackson, Mississippi, was "reasonable" in order to attract new police officers and keep them on the force. Therefore, while enabling older workers to sue under the disparate impact claim, the Supreme Court made it much tougher for them to prove their case. They had to show that an employer's decision was not "reasonable." Making a decision for a reasonable business purpose, such as saving money, is justified under the law.

In another case, the Supreme Court dealt with the issue of reverse age discrimination. In Falls Church, Virginia, the United Auto Workers sued General Dynamics Corporation. The company decided to continue providing retiree medical benefits to workers age fifty and older but to eliminate them for all younger employees. This meant that workers between forty and fifty—who are protected from discrimination under the ADEA—would not receive retiree medical benefits. The Supreme Court ruled that the ADEA was only designed to protect older workers, not younger employees.

According to Jerry Geisel of *Business Insurance*, the "ruling prevents what could have been a slew of litigation against employers, which for decades have designed and offered a wide array of benefit plans that offer more

generous benefits to older employees. Some of those programs include early retirement incentives, in which employers, to encourage older employees to retire and avoid
layoffs, give extra benefits, such as additional pension
[money] to employees over a certain age." Many companies provide these retirement programs so higher-paid
older workers can leave their jobs and be replaced by
lower-paid younger employees. These programs are perfectly legal as a way for organizations to save money.

Baby Boom Workers

Workers born from 1946 to 1964 are part of what is
called the Baby Boom generation. As these workers age—
reaching sixty or older—many of them face age discrimination in the workplace. Indeed, the number of age
discrimination cases brought to the EEOC rose more than
24 percent in the first decade of the twenty-first century.
The large aircraft manufacturer McDonnell-Douglas was
forced to pay $36 million to a group of employees who
charged the company had fired them to reduce its pension
and medical benefit expenses.

The focus of the ADEA is older workers who are fired
simply because of their age. In the past, workers were required to retire by age sixty-five. This was not a problem
for employees during the early part of the twentieth century. Most people were considered old by age sixty-five
and died soon afterward or during their seventies. But advances in health care have made it possible for people to
live longer. Many employees remain vigorous and capable
of doing their work effectively well past age sixty-five. Indeed, they often bring experience to the workplace that
younger employees do not possess. As a result, the ADEA
has eliminated a mandatory retirement age for most jobs.

Nevertheless, American society often seems to regard

How the Government
Resolves Conflicts

Very few cases involving workers' rights ever reach the U.S.
Supreme Court. Many are resolved by the Equal Employment
Opportunity Commission (EEOC). Usually an employee has up to
180 days to file a charge with the EEOC. In each case, workers
must explain why they believe that they have been the victims of
discrimination. Once the EEOC receives the report, known as a
brief, it informs the employer, who must respond by presenting
a brief explaining its side of the case. After reviewing both
briefs, the members of the EEOC may decide that the employer
had not intended to violate that worker's rights, and that it simply occurred out of a misunderstanding.

At this point, the EEOC will try to resolve the matter. But with
less clear-cut conflicts, the EEOC will begin to investigate. The
commission members may talk to witnesses and record their
views of what happened in the case. These witnesses may present conflicting testimony that tells widely differing stories. As a
result, the EEOC must consider the different viewpoints and decide whether a worker's rights have been violated. The violation
may be covered by the Civil Rights Act of 1964, the Age Discrimination Act, the Americans with Disabilities Act, or other
laws covering discrimination. At this point, the commission may
decide that there is no case and the employer has not violated
that worker's rights.

If there is a case, the EEOC will try to resolve the issue. If this
does not work, the commission may decide to take action
against the employer in the form of a lawsuit. But this does not
happen very often. Instead, the EEOC issues a "right to sue let-
ter," enabling a worker to take the issue to court. Court cases
are generally quite costly and may not result in a verdict in favor
of the employee. As a result, a worker may appeal the verdict to
a higher court. Some of these cases eventually reach the U.S.
Supreme Court.

gray-haired workers as less desirable employees. Indeed, the emphasis throughout American culture generally seems to be on youth. Young people are featured in commercials, on magazine covers, and in many films and television programs. Meanwhile, older Americans are often pushed to the sidelines. They are unfairly seen as less flexible in adapting to change and less capable of learning new skills. Once laid off, they often face a difficult task in finding new employment.

Most workers are employed "at will." In the nineteenth century the courts ruled that an employee worked at the will of the employer and could be fired for "good cause, for no cause or even for cause morally wrong, without being thereby guilty of legal wrong." This type of discrimination gave employers power over the hiring and firing of their workers. Gradually unions changed this situation during the twentieth century. However, as unions declined during the late twentieth century, workers were left with little or no protection. At this time, "at will" firings remain very much in force in most states. Federal legislation was passed to protect workers' rights and prevent discrimination. These laws include the ADEA. Without the ADEA, older workers would have little or no protection.

Nevertheless, the rights of workers must be balanced against their employers' rights to remain competitive in the marketplace.

6
Safety in the Workplace

In 1911 the Triangle Shirtwaist Company was doing business on the top floors of the tall Asch Building, located in downtown New York City. Women garment workers were crammed into the dark, dusty sweatshop run by Triangle, where they sewed clothing for fourteen hours a day, receiving only $1.50 per week. On March 25 a fire broke out on the eighth floor of the building, where women were busy stitching clothing. The women on the eighth floor had time to react and began to evacuate the building, but those working on the ninth floor were not told of the fire. By the time they realized what was happening, flames had already spread to the hallway outside their work area, so that exit was blocked and there were no fire extinguishers available to put out the blaze. The only other door had been bolted shut by the company to keep workers inside and at their jobs. As frantic workers tried to save themselves, the fire escape outside the building broke. In a vain effort to escape, some of the women plunged out windows, as

ACCIDENTS

LAD FELL TO DEATH IN BIG COAL CHUTE

Dennis McKee Dead and Arthur Allbecker Had Leg Burned In the Lee Mines.

"Children are not equipped by experience to care for themselves in modern industry"

AND SO THEY PAY

WITH A MAIMED LIFE

Three times as many industrial accidents occur to children as to adults

EMPLOYMENT OF CHILDREN IS DUE TO

IGNORANCE
GREED   OF INDUSTRY AND PARENTS
NECESSITY

ARE ANY OF THESE REASONS WORTH A CHILD'S LIFE?

IN THE EARLY TWENTIETH CENTURY, CHILDREN AS YOUNG AS SIX WERE PUT TO WORK. MANY WERE MAIMED OR KILLED IN FACTORIES AND OTHER JOBS REQUIRING MANUAL LABOR.

horrified pedestrians on the street below watched them fall to their deaths. In all, 146 garment workers died.

Triangle Fire and Workers' Compensation

After the Triangle Shirtwaist Factory fire, Rose Schneiderman helped organize members of the International Ladies Garment Workers Union and led them in a strike in 1913. She fought to outlaw sweatshop labor where workers were exploited and endangered. "I would be a traitor to those poor burned bodies if I came here to talk good fellowship. . . . Every year thousands of us are maimed. The life of men and women is so cheap and property is so sacred," she said at a meeting of New York workers. As a result of the fire, labor leaders in New York began an effort to win passage of new laws that would cover workers who suffered injury or death on the job. Over the next few decades, every state enacted workmen's compensation laws. Under these laws, every employer had to carry insurance that paid employees if they were injured on the job and lost time at work. This amount varies from state to state. "Workers' comp," as it is called, also reimburses workers for medical payments. If a worker is killed on the job, workers' compensation insurance provides benefits to the employee's family.

While workers' compensation provides essential protection for employees against injury on the job, the system can easily be abused. Some employees put in false claims for workers' comp, collecting hundreds or thousands of dollars from their employers. This increases the rates that employers must pay for their insurance. As a result, some employers hire investigators to check up on employees who claim that they cannot report for work because of injuries. In a few instances, employees who said that they were unable to work were videotaped mowing their lawns or playing sports with their friends.

Safety Regulations

While states were enacting workers' compensation laws, they were also requiring employers to follow stricter safety regulations at the workplace. These included new fire codes to avoid a repetition of the Triangle disaster and metal guards positioned on dangerous machinery to insure that workers were not injured by sticking their hands into gears or other machine parts. Employers doing business with the federal government were also required to increase worker safety measures or lose their contracts. Under pressure from the large labor unions, Congress passed the Occupational Safety and Health Act in 1970. The new act established the Occupational Safety and Health Administration (OSHA) to create safety guidelines, inspect workplaces to ensure that employers were following these guidelines, and to fine those organizations that violated them. In addition, the new act established the National Institute of Occupational Safety (NIOSH) to carry on research and testing and establish new guidelines as they became necessary.

Since the Triangle Shirtwaist fire, safety conditions in the workplace have changed radically. In 1913 reports told of 23,000 workers killed on their jobs each year—approximately 61 deaths per 100,000 workers. In the early twenty-first century, that number had dropped to fewer than 7,000 deaths annually—about 4 deaths per 100,000 workers. The largest number of these deaths occurs from highway accidents while workers are transporting materials. Other fatalities result from falls, fires and explosions, breathing harmful substances in the workplace, and being hit by falling objects.

Each year about 1.3 million cases of sickness and injury occur in the workplace. About 40 percent of these are due to spraining a wrist or ankle or straining a muscle. Workers who carry heavy items or drive large tractor-trailers are most likely to receive these injuries.

Much of the improvement in workplace safety is due to more stringent OSHA regulations covering a wide range of potentially dangerous situations. For example, OSHA regulations require that workers handling dangerous chemicals be given a material safety data sheet provided by their employers. These sheets spell out the medical risks from working with certain chemicals if they are not handled properly. The data sheets explain what personal protective gear an employee must wear when handling the chemical. This gear might include a hard hat, safety goggles, a protective suit, rubber boots, and a breathing apparatus. The sheets also explain how to clean up a chemical leak or spill. Other safety procedures spelled out by OSHA explain the proper procedures for working with electrical gear, cleaning machinery, and using scaffolds—high platforms—while painting buildings or working on bridges.

Sometimes, workers are injured or die because they fail to follow the safety guidelines. But according to author Jordan Barab, most deaths result from "a failure of the employer to address well-recognized unsafe workplace conditions and implement effective safety programs in their workplaces. Saving workers' lives is . . . about better enforcement of the Occupational Safety and Health Act." As Barab explained, OSHA has approximately 2,100 inspectors who are responsible for policing 8 million employers. At that rate it would take 115 years for them to cover all of these workplaces.

Currently, OSHA inspects only about 38,000 workplaces annually. If inspectors find a violation, they can write up an employer and issue a fine. These fines can range as high as $70,000 for very serious violations that can cause grave injuries to workers. As a result, workplace injuries have declined by over 60 percent since 1971. Nevertheless, some employers continue to be cited year after year for violations. They would rather pay the fines than change the methods that they use to conduct business. These employers emphasize productivity, higher profits, and keeping their costs as low as possible, not workplace safety.

Among these employers is Tyler Pipe, located on Route 69 in Tyler, Texas. Forty-eight-year-old Rolan Hoskin was one of the employees at the company, which molds huge pipes used to carry water and drain sewage. On June 29, 2000, Hoskin had been directed to repair a conveyor belt on a large molding machine. OSHA regulations stated that the conveyor belt should be stopped during repair work and metal safety guards should be in place to prevent an employee like Hoskin from getting caught in the machine. But there were no safety guards and the belt kept running while Hoskin worked on the machine. Workers interviewed at the plant said there was "less downtime that way," according to *New York Times* reporters David Barstow and Lowell Bergman. Hoskin fell into the machine while it was running, crushing his skull. "If he fought that machine I know his last thought was me," his daughter recalled after hearing of his death.

Tyler Pipe is a subsidiary of a much larger company called McWane Inc., headquartered in Birmingham, Alabama. According to Barstow and Bergman, who talked to employees and OSHA inspectors, all safety regulations have "been subordinated to production, to the commandment to keep the pipe rolling off the line." As one former manager at Tyler Pipe explained, "You put people at risk. We did every day." Workers put in twelve-hour days,

OSHA INSPECTORS FOUND THAT THE TYLER PIPE IRON FOUNDATION IN TYLER, TEXAS, DID NOT FOLLOW MANY SAFETY REGULATIONS REQUIRED BY LAW.

sometimes working seven-day weeks in hot, noisy, dusty conditions. But Tyler is one of the major employers in an area where there are few jobs.

Although the company said it was interested in safety, OSHA inspectors saw something quite different. "They have never developed a mechanism to hold supervisors accountable for safety while, on the other hand, they have mastered a system for holding supervisors accountable for production downtime," according to OSHA inspectors. Although many workers quit, they were replaced by new employees—often inexperienced workers like Rolan Hoskin—who needed jobs.

In 2003 another plant owned by McWane, Atlantic States Cast Iron Pipe, located in New Jersey, was cited for safety violations. Alfred E. Coxe, an employee at the plant, was killed by a forklift with faulty breaks that had never been fixed. When OSHA investigated the incident, managers "took steps to conceal facts," according to an indictment—a legal case—brought against McWane. The managers also told an employee "to provide a misleading account" to OSHA and not tell inspectors about forklifts with safety problems that had never been solved. As at Tyler Pipe, employees in the plant were afraid to disobey their employer because they needed jobs. Nevertheless, the plant manager and other plant supervisors at Atlantic States Cast Iron Pipe were eventually arrested.

The New Jersey case is unusual. Federal safety inspectors generally do not try to prosecute companies or arrest their managers who are responsible for safety violations that lead to an employee's death. In an investigation of over 1,200 workplace deaths that occurred between 1982 and 2002, which OSHA inspectors said were willful safety violations—not violations that were unknown to the employer—only 7 percent of the cases were prosecuted. Instead, OSHA issues citations and fines. These fines totaled $106 million, but in only a few cases were employers prosecuted and sent to jail.

One former OSHA administrator, John T. Phillips, called it "a simple lack of guts and political will." But another administrator, John B. Miles Jr., countered, "We make sure we have the evidence [before we act]." OSHA investigators spend many hours talking to witnesses before deciding to call a violation "willful." The fines are high and the employer's reputation suffers. The decision to pass

ON THE EVENING OF JANUARY 4, 2006, A CANDLELIGHT VIGIL WAS HELD AT THE SAGO BAPTIST CHURCH FOR THE TWELVE WORKERS WHO DIED IN A MINE EXPLOSION AT THE SAGO MINE IN WEST VIRGINIA.

on the case to federal prosecutors is made only as a last resort. "[If] you start accusing people of crimes and they get acquitted," explained former Labor Department official Thomas Williamson Jr., then "you're going to destroy the credibility of the agency." Jeff Brooks, a former OSHA inspector, said OSHA avoided prosecutions except in rare cases. "It can't just be willful, it has to be obscenely willful. . . . If they didn't purposely with malice seek to kill this person, then you don't prosecute."

Yet, more cases may be prosecuted in the future. In 2005 the U.S. Department of Justice, along with OSHA and the Environmental Protection Agency, stated that they were working together to increase their efforts to prosecute employers guilty of gross safety violations.

Indeed, efforts had already begun even before this announcement. In 2001, for example, three officers of a company called LCP Chemicals were found guilty of "knowingly exposing employees to hazardous materials." These workers were burned by mercury and hydrochloric acid. Each of the officers was sentenced to four to nine years in jail. In 2005 Motiva Enterprises paid a $10 million fine after one of its oil tanks exploded, killing one employee and injuring others. A year later Thomas Industrial Coatings was fined $2.3 million for thirty-three willful safety violations. The company was inspected and fined after two workers fell to their deaths from faulty scaffolding while they were working on a bridge. Jail terms and large fines generally occur only after workers are killed.

Mine Safety

In 1969, a year before OSHA was passed, the Federal Mine Safety and Health Administration (MSHA) was established. This occurred after a mine explosion at a coal mine in Farmington, West Virginia, resulted in the deaths

Silicosis

While safety claims by miners and other workers are often valid, sometimes they are not legitimate. An example is silicosis. Silicosis is a severe lung disease that can be fatal. The illness is caused by inhaling fine particles of sand. Workers may develop silicosis while they are drilling in mines or sandblasting to remove waste material that has built up in oil tanks and inside the hulls of ships. To protect themselves, workers are required to wear breathing equipment over their noses and mouths. As a result of safety guidelines issued during the 1970s, the number of silicosis cases was greatly reduced, although many workers still suffered from the disease.

Suddenly in 2002 several thousand new cases were filed in Mississippi by people claiming that they had developed silicosis. Lawyers in the state had run television commercials and newspaper ads looking for any workers who thought they might have silicosis and offering to represent them in lawsuits. The lawsuits threatened to bankrupt U.S. Silica, a large sand manufacturer. According to CEO John Ulizio, "We kind of scratched our heads and figured, 'What the heck's going on down there?' We kind of knew, almost as a matter of course, that they weren't real cases . . . because, if you look at the . . . data on silicosis, there was no indication in the disease prevalence data that there was all of a sudden an epidemic of silicosis."

Delford Zarse, a plumber, saw the commercials. "I was talking to some guy who'd done this, and he said he'd collected quite a bit of money, and I saw these ads in the paper, so I signed up" with a lawyer. "Most of these people didn't go to their doctor first and get a diagnosis of silicosis, then go find a lawyer," said Fred Durtz, who represents the employers being sued. "They went to a screening and got a lawyer first." Lawyers use screening companies and their doctors to run the tests, turning up thousands of claims.

In the past, companies had often offered financial settlements, but in Mississippi they refused and went to court. Federal judge Janis Jack, who heard the case, decided that each of the 10,000 cases being brought should be reexamined. During the reexaminations, massive numbers of errors were found. The doctors who examined the patients for silicosis were questioned in court by the judge, and they changed many of their diagnoses. As a result, the judge threw the cases out of court. She said they had been "manufactured for money."

of seventy-eight miners. After MSHA was established, safety regulations improved, inspections rose, and many violations were eliminated. From two hundred deaths annually in 1969, mining fatalities had dropped to twenty-two in 2005.

MSHA has the power to issue citations and impose penalties, like OSHA. Nevertheless, this is not always enough to prevent disaster. In January 2006 two mining tragedies occurred in West Virginia. Twelve miners were killed in an explosion at the Sago Mine; during the same month, two more miners died in a fire at the Alma Mine. Sago had been cited repeatedly by mine inspectors for safety violations. In 2005 there were more than two hundred violations, and sixty-eight in 2004. But the fines were small—$250 each—to fix problems like controlling natural methane gas that increases during the winter months and can result in explosions.

When the explosion occurred at Sago, the miners were trapped in the mine. They had breathing devices that provided only a short supply of oxygen. They also lacked any cell phones or electronic tracking gear to help rescuers find them. The mine owners also waited two hours to report the disaster. The United Mine Workers union had called for disasters to be reported within fifteen minutes, as well as better breathing and tracking gear for all miners. But nothing had been done by the federal government. According to the PBS *NewsHour with Jim Lehrer*, "Seventy-two Canadian miners were able to walk out of a potash mine after a fire because they had holed up in an underground safe room the company had constructed. U.S. law authorizes MSHA to order safe rooms be built in U.S. mines, but the agency has never issued such an order."

MSHA had also turned down the idea of underground wireless communication for miners that has saved the lives of many miners in other mines. Acting Director David Dye said, "Well, I talked to my tech support folks about that and there are . . . some miners that use it. Some of them, candidly, are enthusiastic about it. Some of them have had a number of problems, including reliability issues."

Meanwhile, MSHA enforcement operations seem to be declining. In 2003 a report from the federal government stated that "although about 44 percent of MSHA's underground coal mine inspectors will be eligible to retire in the next five years, the agency has no plan for replacing them . . . the potential shortage of inspectors may limit MSHA's ability to ensure the safety and health of underground coal miners."

7
Rights of Immigrant Workers

In November 2006 a strike broke out at the Smithfield Packing Company's meat processing plant in Tar Heel, North Carolina, as an estimated five hundred workers refused to go to their jobs. The workers went on strike, in part, because they wanted a union, which had been strongly opposed by Smithfield. In the past, when workers had tried to organize a union, the company fired several of the employees leading the movement, arranged for others to be arrested, and made physical threats against still other workers.

In addition, employees at Smithfield were protesting the working conditions inside the plant. According to Human Rights Watch, "meatpacking is the most dangerous factory job in America." To slice meat into sizes ready for packaging, workers "make up to 30,000 hard-cutting motions with sharp knives, causing massive repetitive motion injuries and frequent lacerations [cuts and wounds]. Workers often do not receive compensation for workplace

WORKERS AT THE PERDUE FARMS INC. PROCESSING PLANT PREPARE CLEANED AND GUTTED CHICKENS FOR PACKAGING. MANY OF THESE EMPLOYEES ARE POORLY PAID IMMIGRANTS.

injuries because companies fail to report injuries, delay and deny claims, and take reprisals [action] against workers who file them."

Another reason that employees at Smithfield went on strike was to protest the firing of immigrant workers whom the company said had entered the country illegally. Under the 1986 Immigration Reform and Control Act (IRCA), employers are supposed to report illegal workers and fire them. Otherwise, the companies could be fined by the government. At Smithfield, managers discovered that some workers had submitted false social security numbers. When these were sent into the Social Security Administration, there were no records of the employees or their numbers. Without valid social security numbers, employees are not permitted to work in the United States.

The meat and poultry industry employs many immigrants in its processing plants. Some of these workers have entered the United States legally. They may have guest worker visas that permit immigrants to work temporarily in industries such as meat packing, forestry, and agriculture. If they leave their jobs, however, they must return to their own countries or be deported by the American government. Other immigrants may have green cards, entitling them to remain in the United States as permanent residents, but without the rights of citizens.

Approximately 140,000 green cards are given to immigrants each year. These immigrants must be sponsored by members of their families who then provide financial support for them. Many immigrants with green cards eventually become American citizens. Still others—approximately 12 million—are illegal immigrants, who enter the United States without permission. Many of them cross the border illegally from Mexico and other nations in Latin America.

In the meat and poultry industry, legal and illegal immigrants often work together. Indeed, they may be members of the same families. Although wages are low in the meat processing field, the pay is better than most workers receive in Mexico or in other Latin American countries. Therefore, immigrants cross the border by the thousands, often to join other family members already working in the United States. According to one estimate, the number of illegal immigrants has grown by one-quarter since 2000.

Human Rights Watch has discovered that employers regularly take advantage of immigrant workers, whether they are in the United States legally or illegally. Since they do not speak much English, legal immigrants who get injured on the job hesitate to contact OSHA because they don't understand the procedure and may be easily persuaded by their employers to remain quiet. As one OSHA official revealed, these workers "just don't know that they have rights and responsibilities." Illegal immigrants are easily pressured by employers who threaten to fire them and have them deported if they complain about working conditions.

According to one beef worker,

> **If you hurt your back or your shoulder, something they can't see, you go see the nurse. She tells you there's nothing wrong and gives you Tylenol and says go back to work. If you're still hurting they send you to the company doctor. He says you didn't hurt yourself in the plant, go back to work. Then you go see a lawyer to file a claim. On the paper it says you have to sign your real name and swear to it. A lot of people stop right there. Their work name is not their real name.**

They are here illegally. As a result, employers argue that these illegal immigrants are not required to receive workers' compensation.

Migrant Workers

Similar conditions exist in the agricultural industry. Thousands of immigrant workers are employed in the fields doing the backbreaking work of picking fruits and vegetables. In addition, they are exposed to pesticides that protect the crops from insects but infect agricultural workers. As many as 300,000 workers get sick from pesticides each year. Agricultural workers are often called migrants because they move from one farm to another, harvesting a variety of crops. Some of them work in Florida and travel northward along the East Coast, from one state to another, where the harvesting season occurs later and later. About 65 percent of the workers come from Mexico.

Entire families travel together, living in cramped, run-down motel rooms because that is all that they can afford. Sometimes as many as ten people live in a single room. Workers average about $5,000 to $7,500 per year from their employers. Most of them receive no health care benefits or workers' compensation if they become sick or get injured. As reporter Christine Ahn explained,

> **Growers claim that a shortage of legal workers willing to do farm labor forces them to hire undocumented workers, whose fear of deportation often stops them from challenging low wages and poor working and housing conditions. An example of this downward wage pressure can be seen in wages paid to tomato pickers. In 1980, they earned minimum wage by picking just over seven buckets of tomatoes. By 1997, pickers had to fill thirteen buckets. Today, in Immokalee, Florida, the fastest tomato pickers must fill between 100–150 buckets to earn $40–$60 a day, while slower pickers who fill 70–80 buckets earn only $28 a day. During**

the harvest season, tomato pickers work seven days a week, 10–12 hours daily, and earn just $7,500.

This is less than the federal minimum wage, which currently is $5.15 per hour. According to U.S. law, workers should also be entitled to time and a half for overtime—one and one-half times the normal hourly wage for every hour over forty that they work each week—but many employers do not pay them these wages.

Migrant workers face the same problems whether they are legal or illegal immigrants. Global Horizons, a California company, brought workers from Thailand into Washington State to pick produce in its bountiful orchards, which grow apples and other fruit. The Thai workers were given guest worker visas, enabling them to work legally in the United States. Although employees were promised a specific rate of pay from Global Horizons, an investigation by the U.S. Department of Labor revealed that the company had not fulfilled its agreements with the workers. Moreover, Global Horizons put the workers in run-down housing—far below the type of housing conditions that the company had promised. Washington State fruit growers threatened to end their relationship with Global Horizons. To prevent this situation, the company agreed to let their employees join a union. The United Farm Workers (UFW) union, founded in 1973, had won many agreements with growers to provide better working conditions in the agricultural industry. As a result of a new contract, the Thai workers won an increase in pay and guaranteed health insurance.

In addition to agriculture, guest workers are also employed in landscaping and forestry. Many enter the United States from Mexico, Guatemala, and other nations in Latin America. In the forestry industry, guest workers cut

The Debate on Minimum Wage Laws

In 1938 Congress passed the Fair Labor Standards Act (FLSA), establishing a minimum wage for employees in the workplace. The wage was only twenty-five cents per hour. In 2006 the minimum wage was $5.15 per hour, the same rate as in 1997. Under FLSA, workers are supposed to receive time and a half—one and one-half times the minimum wage for every hour worked over eight hours—and double time for working more than twelve hours daily. The law applies to all workers who are not exempt under the FLSA, such as executives, secretaries, and other administrative personnel. But some employers misclassify employees as exempt to avoid paying them overtime.

Meanwhile, as the cost of living has risen, the value of the minimum wage has declined by almost 30 percent since 1979. Congress has not authorized an increase in the federal minimum wage since 1997. During the 1990s states were given the right to raise the minimum wage over the amount set by the federal government. Eighteen states had set their minimum wage rates higher than the federal level by 2006.

Congress regularly debates whether the minimum wage should be raised, considering arguments for and against making increases. Those who argue for increases state that workers should be paid fairly—that is, enough to afford food, clothing, and housing. Without a fair wage, they say, workers will be exploited by employers who will pay them as little as possible. Yet, if more money is in the hands of employees, they will make a larger contribution to the economy by purchasing more items. In addition, these workers will not need to go on welfare and receive money from the government to afford to live.

However, those who argue against increases in the minimum wage point out that many businesses cannot afford to pay their workers higher wages. As a result, these workers would be laid off from their jobs. Also, a higher minimum wage might hurt younger workers in entry level jobs. They are currently paid the minimum wage and if it were increased, employers couldn't afford to hire them. Meanwhile, any employers who could afford to pay the increase in minimum wages would be likely to raise the prices on the goods that they sell, making them more expensive for consumers.

down old trees that are turned into lumber for housing. They also plant new trees to replace them. The work is often dangerous. According to writer Kari Lydersen, "These workers wield chainsaws and dodge falling trees in snow and rain; carry heavy packs of seeds and pound shovels into rocky ground for hours on end; and often spend nights sleeping on tarps on the forest floor." The wages are low, less than the minimum wage, and the workers are required to plant two thousand new seedlings daily. As Mary Bauer of the Southern Poverty Law Center explains, "Everybody in the industry uses [guest] workers, and everybody in the industry underpays them."

Debating Immigrant Rights

The rights of immigrant workers have become a hotly debated topic in the United States. In 2004 President George W. Bush proposed a new plan to change the laws that currently apply to illegal immigrant workers. He said that "some of the jobs being generated in America's growing economy are jobs American citizens are not filling." Instead, employers are relying on illegal workers to do these jobs. President Bush proposed that these workers should identify themselves and they could join a temporary program for three years. After this period, the workers could then apply to have their temporary status extended for another three-year period. "This new system will be more compassionate," President Bush added.

> **Decent, hardworking people will now be protected by labor laws, with the right to change jobs, earn fair wages, and enjoy the same working conditions that the law requires for American workers. . . . Temporary workers will be able to establish their identities by obtaining the legal documents that we**

**all take for granted. And they will be able to talk
openly to authorities to report crimes when
they're harmed without the fear of being deported.**

Several U.S. senators have proposed to go even further
than President Bush. They suggest that illegal immigrants
should not only receive guest visas but should eventually
be given the opportunity to remain in the United States
and become full citizens. In addition, the Senate proposals
would provide more green cards for immigrants annually.
These proposals would have the greatest impact in states
such as Arizona, California, and Florida, where there are
large numbers of illegal immigrants working in agriculture
and other industries. In Arizona alone there are almost
half a million illegal immigrants. Currently, these immigrants might pay $150 to obtain a phony social security
card and a green card, enabling them to be hired by employers without seeming to violate the immigration laws.

Many lawmakers, however, oppose any attempt to
legalize the status of illegal immigrants by passing new legislation. They label such proposals "amnesty"—a reward
for illegal workers violating the law if they now come forward and reveal themselves. However, the IRCA of 1986
gave amnesty to thousands of illegal workers who had entered the United States before the law was passed and then
came forward to admit their status.

Those opposed to amnesty propose that illegal immigrants should be rounded up and deported from the
United States. They claim that many employers hire illegal
immigrant workers and pay them in cash to avoid report-
ing any earnings to the government and paying the social
security taxes. They emphasize that these workers and
their families use the emergency rooms of hospitals when
they are injured, paying little or nothing for the service.
Because their families are poor, they receive food stamps—

free coupons used to pay for food in supermarkets—and other welfare benefits, without paying taxes. Although the workers do not pay taxes, their children attend American schools, which are supported by taxpayer dollars. According to one estimate, illegal immigrants cost the United States $10 billion more than they spend in the economy each year.

Finally, opponents of new proposals charge that illegal immigrant workers do not fill jobs that American citizens do not want. Instead, they are willing to work for lower pay, thus pushing aside U.S. citizens who want to be paid the minimum wage or higher. In addition, by accepting lower wages, these immigrants keep down the wages that American citizens—competing with illegal immigrants for the same jobs—might earn in the workplace.

In contrast, advocates of providing changes in the status of illegal immigrants point out that 75 percent of them have taxes taken out of their paychecks by employers. This money is contributed to social security and Medicare for retirees. However, since most illegal immigrants return to their home countries before retirement, they do not receive any of the benefits of retirement programs. According to one estimate, illegal workers contribute $7 billion per year to retirement programs, but receive none of the benefits when they retire.

Nevertheless, many Americans want to keep illegal immigrants from entering the United States. In 2006 Congress voted to build a 700-mile fence along the U.S. border with Mexico as a way of reducing the numbers of immigrants who cross illegally. The U.S. Border Patrol has stepped up efforts to prevent illegal immigrants from crossing into the Southwest. Groups of volunteers have begun patrolling the border, keeping an eye out for illegal immigrants and stopping them from entering the United States. States such as California and Arizona have also

TWO MEXICAN MEN LOOK OVER THE U.S.–MEXICO BORDER BEFORE A 2005 NEWS CONFERENCE CONCERNING LEGISLATION THAT WOULD HAVE ALLOWED THE U.S. BORDER PATROL TO FORTIFY THE WESTERN-MOST STRETCH OF THE BORDER.

passed legislation preventing illegal immigrants from using schools and hospitals, or receiving welfare because of the high costs to taxpayers.

However, some economists point out that by arresting illegal workers, law enforcement officials just damage the U.S. economy. Since the wages earned by illegal immigrants are less than those paid to other workers, consumer prices remain low. In addition, employers have more money available to hire highly skilled workers who traditionally receive much higher wages. Many immigrants work in the home-building industry. As one builder explained, "If I'm a builder and I can hire more wallboard guys [unskilled workers who nail on walls] cheaply, my [ability to use] skilled carpenters goes up."

Employers are supposed to check the paperwork that immigrants present upon being hired. This includes social security cards and visas. Each year Tommy Brock, who grows strawberries and tomatoes in Florida, hires over one hundred immigrants to pick his produce. "I haven't hired anybody without doing all the proper paperwork for over fifteen years," he said. But as Susan Ladika, a reporter for *HR Magazine*, pointed out, "There's currently no widespread, reliable system in place that Brock—or countless other employers—can use to see if the documents they receive are legitimate." Marlene Colucci, executive vice president for public policy at the American Hotel & Lodging Association, adds that turning down a prospective employee when "his documents don't seem in order could expose the employer to a discrimination investigation or a lawsuit if the worker's paperwork is indeed valid."

On the other hand, if employers hire an illegal immigrant, they may face stiffer penalties than in the past. Previously, an employer was charged with a small fine. More recently, however, the U.S. Department of Homeland Security has begun arresting employers who regularly hire illegal immigrants. During the first half of 2006, an estimated 445 employers were arrested, as compared with 176 in all of 2005. According to assistant secretary Julie Myers of U.S. Immigration and Customs Enforcement (ICE), they are "taking an increasingly tough stance against . . . corporate violators that knowingly employ illegal aliens. This is a wholesale departure from the past system of sanctioning [punishing] corporate violators with minor fines, which were rarely paid in a timely manner or at all." In Kentucky, two companies that run hotels paid $1.5 million in fines in July 2006 for allowing illegal immigrants to work for them. Earlier that same year authorities arrested over 1,100 people at IFCO Systems—a nationwide manufacturing company—for employing illegal immigrants.

Illegal immigrants who work in the hotel and restaurant industry or for building contractors often gather early in the morning at community sites where they are hired as day laborers. In some towns, however, residents have become angry about having groups of immigrants congregating in their community and creating a nuisance. As a result, town officials in communities such as Mamaroneck, New York, a wealthy suburb of New York City, "waged a discriminatory campaign of ticketing and harassment to drive Latino day laborers out of town," according to the *New York Times*. Similar actions had occurred in Freehold, New Jersey, and Redondo Beach, California. In May 2006 a federal court in California ruled that authorities in Redondo Beach could no longer arrest day workers who were looking for work. In November a court in New York ordered Mamaroneck to stop its harassment of day laborers.

Nevertheless, the California court's decision points out the difficulty of dealing with problems created by illegal immigrants. As reported in the *New York Times*, "while the courts have upheld the basic rights of an abused

MEXICAN MIGRANT WORKERS COMPETE FOR JOBS AS DAY LABORERS EVERY DAY.

minority, they have not made day laborers any more welcome in their communities or helped local governments find ways to treat them with dignity while upholding residents' desires for a reasonable amount of order." This would require new immigration laws.

Maria-Cinta Lowe, executive director of the Hispanic Center of Greater Danbury, Connecticut, explained, "The system is broken, really, really broken. The federal government has got to fix it." In Danbury, officials estimate that there are between 10,000 and 20,000 illegal immigrants.

As the debate over immigration laws continues, the status of immigrant workers and their rights remains an important issue that hangs in the balance.

Chronology

1806
Philadelphia cordwainers are charged with conspiracy for striking.

1840
Federal government establishes ten-hour day for workers.

1842
Massachusetts rules that labor unions are not illegal.

1867
Order of the Knights of Saint Crispin is formed.

1869
Knights of Labor union is formed.

1881
American Federation of Labor (AFL) union begins.

1892
Homestead Strike occurs in Pennsylvania.

1914–1918
World War I is fought; union membership grows.

1929
Great Depression begins.

1932
Franklin Roosevelt becomes president of the
United States.

1933
National Industrial Recovery Act recognizes unions.

1935
Wagner Act strengthens the power of unions.

1938
Congress passes Fair Labor Standards Act, establishing
a minimum wage.

1938
Congress of Industrial Organizations (CIO) is formed.

1939–1945
World War II is fought.

1964
Civil Rights Act is passed.

1965
Medicare is passed; provides health care for retirees.

1967
Congress passes Age Discrimination in Employment Act.

1969
Federal Mine Safety and Health Administration is established.

1970
Occupational Safety and Health Act (OSHA) is enacted.

1978
Congress passes Pregnancy Discrimination Act.

1986
Immigration Reform and Control Act is passed.

1990
Americans with Disabilities Act is enacted.

1992
Health benefits are offered to partners of gay and lesbian workers.

1993
Congress passes Family and Medical Leave Act.

2004
President Bush proposes new plan to help illegal immigrants.

2006
Sago and Alma mine disasters occur.
Congress votes to build fence along United States–Mexican border.

Notes

Chapter 1

Page 8, par. 4, Liza Featherstone, *Selling Women Short* (New York: Basic Books, 2004), p. 5.

Page 9, par. 1, *Frontline*, "Is Wal-Mart Good for America?" November 16, 2004. http://www.pbs.org/wgbh/pages/frontline/shows/walmart/etc/synopsis.html

Page 9, par. 2, ibid.

Page 9, par. 3, ibid.

Page 10, par. 1, Milt Freudenheim, "Side Effects at the Pharmacy," *New York Times*, November 30, 2006.

Page 10, par. 3, *Frontline*.

Page 11, par. 1–page 12, par. 1, Cathleen Flahardy, "Wal-Mart's Labor Woes Teach GCs A Lesson in Law," *Corporate Legal Times*, March 2005, p. 23.

Page 12, par. 3, Michael Maiello, "Wal-Mart Can't Clean Up," *Forbes.com*, October 10, 2005. http://www.forbes.com/business/2005/10/10/lawsuit-immigration-wmt-cz_mm_10 10walmart.html

Chapter 2

Page 18, par. 1, David Brody, *In Labor's Cause* (New York: Oxford University Press, 1993), p. 3.

Page 20, par. 4, Horace M. Eaton, *Report of the Industrial Commission on the Relations of Capital and Labor Employed in Manufactures and General Business*, House Executive Document 495, (Washington, D.C.), pp. 359, 361, 363, 1889.

Page 25, par. 1, Samuel Gompers, *Collective Bargaining* (New York: Dutton, 1920), p. 285.

Page 26, par. 1, Robert Zieger and Gilbert Gall, *American Workers, American Unions* (Baltimore: Johns Hopkins University Press, 2002), p. 4.

Page 26, par. 3, ibid., pp. 12–13.

Page 28, par. 2, ibid., p. 47.

Page 28, par. 3, ibid., p. 63.

Page 29, par. 3, page 31, par. 1, ibid., pp. 80–81.

Page 32, par. 2, ibid., p. 105.

Page 32, par. 2, ibid., p. 108.

Page 33, par. 2, ibid., p. 121.

Page 35, par. 1, ibid., p. 199.

Chapter 3

Page 36, par. 1, Thomas J. Sugrue, "The Compelling Need for Diversity in Higher Education." http://www.vpcomm. umich.edu/admissions/research/expert/sugru10.html

Page 39, par. 2, Francine D. Blau and Anne E. Winkler, "Countering Stereotypes by Changing the Rules," *Regional Review*, 2005.

Page 39, par. 3, ibid.

Page 40, par. 1, ibid.

Page 40, par. 3, Christopher M. Leporini, "Affirmative Action in the Workplace," *American Bar Association*, Spring 1998. http://www.abanet.org/publiced/focus/spr98work. html

Page 41, par. 1, Aaron Bernstein, "Racism in the Workplace," *BusinessWeek*, July 30, 2001. http://www.businessweek. com/print/magazine/content/01_31/b3743084.htm?chan= mz

Page 41, par. 2, ibid.

Page 41, par. 3, "Race Discrimination Suit Targets Coke Bottler CCE," *Atlanta Business Chronicle*, May 5, 2003.

http://atlanta.bizjournals.com/atlanta/stories/2003/05/05/
story1.html?=printable

Page 43, par. 2, Raymond F. Gregory, *Women and Workplace Discrimination* (New Brunswick, NJ: Rutgers University Press, 2003), p. 34.

Page 45, par. 4, ibid., pp. 16–18.

Page 46, par. 1, ibid., p. 74.

Page 46, par. 3–page 47, par. 1, Wendy Harris, "Hidden Bias," *Black Enterprise*, March 2006.

Page 47, par. 2, Mary E. Williams, ed., *Discrimination: Opposing Viewpoints* (San Diego: Greenhaven Press, 2003), p. 43.

Page 48, par. 1, Gregory, *Women and Workplace Discrimination*, p. 124.

Page 48, par. 4, Louise Gerdes, ed., *Sexual Harassment* (San Diego: Greenhaven Press, 1999), p. 18.

Page 49, par. 1, ibid., p. 21.

Chapter 4

Page 50, par. 1, David Moberg, "Labor Fights for Rights," *Nation*, September 15, 2003, p. 25.

Page 54, par. 4–page 55, par. 2, Connecticut Office of Health Care Access, "Who Are The Uninsured?" January, 2003. http://www.ct.gov/ohca/lib/ohca/publications/uninsured coverage4pdf.pdf

Page 55, par. 2, Page 56, par. 3, Stacy Forster, "Tab for Uninsured Workers Rises 13%," *Milwaukee Journal Sentinel*, July 1, 2006.

Page 55, par. 4–page 56, par. 1, The Commonwealth Fund, "A Shared Responsibility: U.S. Employers and the Provision of Health Insurance to Employees," 2006. http://www. cmwf.org/publications/publications_show.htm?doc_id=28 0373

Page 56, par. 2, "Who Are The Uninsured?"

Page 57, par. 1–3, Erik Eckholm, "To Lower Costs, Hospitals Try Free Basic Care for Uninsured," *New York Times*, October 25, 2006. http://query.nytimes.com/gst/fullpage. html?sec=health&res=9C02E6DE143FF936A15753C1A9 609C8B63&n=Top%2fReference%2fTimes%20Topics% 2fPeople%2fE%2fEckholm%2c%20Erik

Page 58, par. 1–2, Institute for Women's Policy Research, "Businesses and Families Suffer Without Sick Leave," May

5, 2004. http://www. iwpr.org/pdf/SickLeavePR5-5-04.pdf

Page 58, par. 3, "Health Insurance Benefits for Domestic Part - ners," Insure.com. http://info.insure.com/health/domestic. html

Page 59, par. 1–2, ibid.

Page 60, par. 1, Vhi Healthcare, "Workplace Discrimination: Sexual Orientation," December 8, 2000. http://www2. vhi.ie/topic/sexordiscrim

Page 61, par. 2, "Examining the Employment Nondiscrimina- tion Act (ENDA): The Scientists Perspective," Apa.org. http://www.apa.org/pi/lgbc/publications/enda.html

Page 62, par. 2, Stephanie Armour, "Family, Medical Leave Act at Center of Hot Debate," *USA Today*, May 25, 2005. http://www.usatoday.com/money/economy/employment/ 2005-05-25-medical-leave-usat_x.htm

Chapter 5

Page 64, par. 1, "Disabled Workers Advance in High-Tech Careers," http://www.employmentguide.com/careeradvice/ Disabled_Workers_Advance.html.

Page 65, par. 1–page 66, par. 1, Naomi Earp, Chair of the EEOC, "Reviewing the Americans with Disabilities Act," FDCH Congressional Testimony, September 13, 2006.

Page 67, par. 1, Workplace Fairness: Court Cases in the News, "Disabled Worker Awarded $4.6 Million," June 23, 2004. http://www.workplacefairness.org/index.php?page=court cases&state=IN&view=print

Page 67, par. 2, Kris Maher, "Disabled Workers Are Finding It Tougher to Secure Employment," *Wall Street Journal*, October 7, 2005. http://www.careerjournal.com/myc/diver sity/20051007-maher.html

Page 68, par. 1, "Cost of Accommodating Disabled Workers Averages Less than $500, New Survey Says," *Bureau of National Affairs* 21, no. 14, April 14, 2003. http://sub script.bna.com/pic2/hr2pic.nsf/id/BNAP-5LLK86?Open Document&PrintVersion=Yes

Page 68, par. 2–3, Paul Vitello, "Home Depot Pays a Disabled Ex-Worker," *New York Times*, October 25, 2005. http:// topics.nytimes.com/top/news/business/companies/home_ depot_inc/index.html?offset=50&

Page 69, par. 1, Graydon Head & Ritchey LLP, Attorneys at

Law, "Disabled Workers Awarded Millions against Wal-Mart." http://www.graydon.com/index.cfm/fuseaction/ne ws_events.newsletter_detail/object_id/c9e951d8-8d64-418 4-9958-7a37af41adcf/DisabledworkerawardedmillionsagainstWalMart.cfm

Page 69, par. 2–page 70, par. 1, "*US Airways, Inc., Petitioner v. Robert Barnett*," April 29, 2002. http://caselaw.lp.find law.com/scripts/getcase.pl?court=US&vol=000&invol=00 1250

Page 70, par. 2–page 71, par. 1, Kate Randall and John Andrews, "U.S. Supreme Court Ruling Limits Disabled Workers' Rights," January 14, 2002. http://www.wsws.org /articles/2002/jan2002/ada-j14.shtml

Page 71, par. 3, Adam Cohen, "Too Old to Work?" *New York Times*, March 2, 2003. http://topics.nytimes.com/top/ reference/timestopics/people/c/adam_cohen/index.html?off set=80&

Page 72, par. 2–3, ibid.

Page 74, par. 2, Morgan Lewis, "*Smith* v. *City of Jackson*: Good News and Bad News For Employers Defending Against Disparate Impact Claims Under the ADEA," April 1, 2005. http://www.morganlewis.com/pubs/Smith%20v. %20City%20of%20Jackson3.pdf

Page 74, par. 4–page 75, par. 1, Jerry Geisel, "Ruling Allows More Generous Benefits for Those over 40 ADEA," *Business Insurance*, March 1, 2004, Au

Page 75, par. 2, Cohen, "Too Old to Work," Au

Chapter 6

Page 80, par. 2, Leon Stein, *The Triangle Fire* (New York: Carrol & Graf, 1962), p. 144.

Page 81, par. 1, Vernon Morgensen, ed., *Worker Safety Under Siege* (Armonk, NY: M. E. Sharpe, 2006), p. xviii.

Page 81, par. 2, ibid., p. 4.

Page 81, par. 3–page 82, par. 1, *Bureau of Labor Statistics News*, "Lost-worktime Injuries and Illnesses: Characteristics and Resulting Time Away from Work." December 13, 2005. http://stats.bls.gov/news.release/archives/osh2_1213 2005.pdf

Page 82, par. 3, Morgensen, *Worker Safety Under Siege*, pp. 13–14.

Page 82, par. 4, U.S. Department of Labor, Occupational Safety & Health Administration, "Frequently Asked Questions." http://www.osha.gov/as/opa/osha-faq.html

Page 83, par. 2–3, page 84, par. 1, David Barstow and Lowell Bergman, "At a Texas Foundry, an Indifference to Life," *New York Times*, January 8, 2003. http://www.nytimes.com/2003/01/08/national/08PIPE.html?ex=1176436800&en=3dd4290a55678e5f&ei=5070

Page 85, par. 1, David Barstow, "Officials at Foundry Face Health and Safety Charges," *New York Times*, sec. A, p. 21, December 16, 2003.

Page 85, par. 2, page 87, par. 1, David Barstow, "U.S. Rarely Seeks Charges for Deaths in Workplace," *New York Times*, December 22, 2003. http://www.nytimes.com/2003/12/22/national/22OSHA.html?ex=1176436800&en=5d09b094f700febd&ei=5070

Page 87, par. 3, Daniel Riesel and Dan Chorost, "New Initiatives Prosecute Workplace-Safety Violations Using Environmental Laws," *Springboard Legal Trends and Analysis*, Summer 2005. http://www.sprlaw.com/pdf/spr_sprngbrd_summer_05.pdf

Page 88, par. 2–page 89, par. 3, Wade Goodwyn, "Silicosis Ruling Could Revamp Legal Landscape," National Public Radio, November 16, 2006. http://www.npr.org/templates/story/story.php?storyId=5244935

Page 90, par. 2, "Coal Towns React to Recent Fatal Accidents," *Online News Hour*, February 1, 2006. http://www.pbs.org/newshour/bb/health/jan-june06/minetown_2-01.html

Page 90, par. 3, ibid.

Page 91, par. 1, Christopher D. Cook, "Coal Miners' Slaughter," *In These Times*, January 25, 2006. http://www.inthesetimes.com/site/main/article/2478/

Chapter 7

Page 92, par. 2, page 94, par. 1, "Abuses Against Workers Taint U.S. Meat and Poultry," Human Rights Watch, January 25, 2005. http://hrw.org/english/docs/2005/01/25/usdom10052.htm

Page 95, par. 1, Shailagh Murray, "Conservatives Split in Debate on Curbing Illegal Immigration," *Washington Post*, March 25, 2005. http://www.washingtonpost.com/wp-dyn/articles/A64179-2005Mar24.html

Page 95, par. 2 and 3, "Immigrant Workers in the United States Meat and Poultry Industry," Human Rights Watch, December 15, 2005. http://www.hrw.org/backgrounder/usa/un-sub1005/

Page 96, par. 3, Christine Ahn, "Migrant Farm Workers: America's New Plantation Workers," *Backgrounder* 10, no. 2, Spring 2004. http://www.foodfirst.org/pubs/backgr drs/2004/sp04v10n2.html

Page 97, pars. 2 and 3, 100, par. 1, Kari Lydersen, "Guest Workers Seek Global Horizons: U.S. Company Exploits Migrant Labor," *Corp Watch*, November 3, 2006. http://www.corpwatch.org/article.php?id=14216

Page 100, par. 2, "Bush Calls for Changes on Illegal Workers," CNN.com, January 8, 2004. http://www.cnn.com/2004/ALLPOLITICS/01/07/bush.immigration/

Page 101, par. 3, "Illegal Immigration Factsheet," New Media Alliance, http://www.therealitycheck.org/StaffWriter/Illegal_ImmigrationFS.html

Page 102, par. 2, Eduardo Porter, "Illegal Immigrants Are Bolstering Social Security with Billions," *New York Times*, sec. A, p.1, April 5, 2005. http://www.nytimes.com/2005/04/05/business/05immigration.html?pagewanted=2&ei=5090&en=78c87ac4641dc383&ex=1270353600

Page 104, par. 2, Chris Isidore, "Illegal Workers: Good for U.S. Economy," CNNMoney.com, May 1, 2006. http://money.cnn.com/2006/05/01/news/economy/immigration_economy/index.htm

Page 104, par. 3, Susan Ladika, "Trouble on the Hiring Front," *HR Magazine*, October 2006. http://www.shrm.org/hrmagazine/articles/1006/1006ladika.asp

Page 104, par. 4–105, par. 1, "Arrests of Employers of Illegal Immigrants on the Rise," *USA Today*, July 22, 2006.

Page 105, pars. 2–3, Editorial, "Day Laborers' Rights," *New York Times*, sec. A, p. 34, November 24, 2006. http://www.truthout.org/cgi-bin/artman/exec/view.cgi/66/24107

Page 105, par. 3, page 107, par. 1, Bob Chuvala, "Feds Crack Down on Illegal Labor in Danbury," *Fairfield County Business Journal*, October 9, 2006. http://www.fairfield-cbj.com/archive/100906/1009060003.php

All Web sites were accessible as of May 18, 2007.

Further Information

Further Reading

Balkin, Karen, ed. *Poverty: Opposing Viewpoints*. San Diego: Greenhaven Press, 2003.

Williams, Mary E., ed. *Discrimination: Opposing Viewpoints*. San Diego: Greenhaven Press, 2003.

Worth, Richard. *Africans in America*. New York: Facts on File, 2005.

———. *Mexican Immigrants*. New York: Facts on File, 2005.

Web Sites

American Bar Association
http://www.abanet.org

BusinessWeek
http://www.businessweek.com

Forbes.com
http://www.forbes.com

New York Times
http://www.nytimes.com

PBS *Frontline*
http://www.pbs.org/frontline

Bibliography

Baxandall, Rosalyn, and Linda Gordon, eds. *America's Working Women: A Documentary History*. New York: W. W. Norton, 1995.

Brody, David. *In Labor's Cause*. New York: Oxford University Press, 1993.

Featherstone, Liza. *Selling Women Short*. New York: Basic Books, 2004.

Gerdes, Louise, ed. *Sexual Harassment*. San Diego: Greenhaven Press, 1999.

Gregory, Raymond. *Unwelcome and Unlawful: Sexual Harassment in the American Workplace*. Ithaca, NY: Cornell University Press, 2004.

——. *Women and Workplace Discrimination*. New Brunswick, NJ: Rutgers University Press, 2003.

Morgensen, Vernon, ed. *Worker Safety under Siege*. Armonk, NY: M. E. Sharpe, 2006.

O'Toole, James, and Edward Lawler. *The New American Workplace*. New York: Palgrave Macmillan, 2006.

Zieger, Robert, and Gilbert Gall. *American Workers, American Unions*. Baltimore: Johns Hopkins University Press, 2002.

Index

Page numbers in **boldface** are illustrations, tables, and charts.

About the Author

Richard Worth is the author of more than fifty books. These include biographies, histories, and books on current events. Among his books are a biography of Ariel Sharon, a history of the slave trade, and the award-winning *Gangs and Crime*. His most recent book for Marshall Cavendish Benchmark was *The Arab-Israeli Conflict* in this series.